Minute Guide to

Effective
Leadership

by Andrew J. DuBrin

Macmillan Spectrum/Alpha Books

A Division of Macmillan General Reference
A Simon & Schuster Macmillan Company
1633 Broadway, New York, NY 10019-6705

International Standard Book Number: 0-02-861406-2
Library of Congress Catalog Card Number: A catalog record of this publication is available through the Library of Congress.

99 98 97   8 7 6 5 4 3 2

Interpretation of the printing code: the rightmost double-digit number is the year of the book's first printing; the rightmost single-digit number is the number of the book's printing. For example, a printing code of 97-1 shows that this copy of the book was printed during the first printing of the book in 1997.

Printed in the United States of America

Publisher: Theresa Murtha

Editor-in-Chief: Richard J. Staron

Production Editor: Linda Seifert

Copy Editors: Mike McFeely and Patty Solberg

Cover Designer: Ann Armstrong

Designer: Glenn Larsen

Indexer: Eric Brinkman

Production Team: Angela Calvert, Tricia Flodder, Rowena Rappaport, Megan Wade

CONTENTS

INTRODUCTION

Did you ever notice that those characteristics and behaviors that we attribute to leaders are similar to those that we attribute to admirable people in general? That's not an accident. We usually feel comfortable around those we admire and they make us feel good about ourselves. So do leaders. But leaders also know what to do to move us to cooperation and productive action. They understand that their role is to pull people together to achieve a goal everyone in the group or organization shares.

Leaders are self-confident and inspire self-confidence in others. Leaders project personal dynamism. Leaders know how to speak in a way that moves others to action. Leaders know how to nurture and coach others. They help others to be more creative. Leaders build teamwork among their followers. But the question is how do they do these things?

First of all, they have a leadership attitude. This is an attitude that tells others that they are not afraid to make decisions and take risks. And it's an attitude that shows they have the best interests of the group in mind.

Second, leaders behave in distinctive ways. An important goal of this book is to help you learn about those distinctive behaviors.

For example, you'll learn some specific things you can do to nurture others. You'll learn how to use language techniques that will move people to action. And you'll learn what to do bring out your people's creative impulses.

Managers must deal with the technical aspects of running a group or organization. Leaders deal with the people aspects. Both skills are necessary to succeed. If you ever wondered exactly what you might do to be perceived as a leader by others, this book answers that question.

As you read this book, try the behaviors suggested. They work. But in doing so, also strive for the leadership attitude. It is one that says "I care more about us than about me." It says "I'm willing to put my own welfare on the line for you." And it says "I understand what needs to be done, and I'm going to help us all succeed."

CONVENTIONS USED IN THIS BOOK

This book uses three icons to help you quickly find important information:

Timesaver Tip icons offer ideas that cut corners and avoid confusion.

Plain English icons define new terms.

Panic Button icons identify potential problem areas and tell you how to solve them.

THE AUTHOR

Dr. Andrew J. DuBrin is a Professor of Management at the College of Business, Rochester Institute of Technology, and a consultant to organizations. He teaches courses in organizational behavior, career management, and leadership. He speaks and leads professional development seminars. Dr. DuBrin received his Ph.D. from Michigan State University in Industrial Psychology.

Dr. DuBrin is the author of numerous textbooks, trade books, and journal and magazine articles. His work has been quoted in such magazines and newspapers as *The Wall Street Journal*, *The New York Times*, and *Working Woman*. He has contributed several articles to *Bottom Line Personal* and *Bottom Line Business*. He is also author of several other books, including *Winning Office Politics*, *Getting It Done: The Transforming Power of Self-Discipline*, and *The Breakthrough Team Player*. He lives in Rochester, New York.

ACKNOWLEDGMENTS

This book came to be because of two people: Dick Staron and John Woods. Dick, editor-in-chief at Macmillan General Reference, commissioned John Woods of CWL Publishing Enterprises to develop this book. John asked me to write it and then supported me throughout the process. I want to thank both of them. And thank you for selecting this book to help you learn about how to be an effective leader.

1

WHAT IT MEANS TO BE A LEADER

In this lesson you will learn the meaning of leadership, and the difference between leadership and management.

THE MEANING OF LEADERSHIP

A starting point in becoming an effective leader is to understand what leadership and being a leader are all about.

Leadership is such an important topic in business as well as in other spheres of life that the term has been defined in many ways. All of these definitions have an important message for the aspiring or practicing leader.

- Leadership is interpersonal influence directed toward attaining goals and achieved through communication.

- Leadership is the influential increment over and above mechanical compliance with directions and orders.

- Leadership is an act that causes others to act or respond in a shared direction.

- Leadership is the art of influencing people by persuasion or example to follow a course of action.

- Leadership is the key dynamic force that motivates and coordinates the organization in the accomplishment of its objectives.

In short, leadership deals with persuading, inspiring, motivating others, and spearheading useful changes. A leader creates a sensible vision for others, and then directs them toward achieving that vision. To be a leader, the people you are attempting to lead must have confidence in you and give you their support and commitment. You need support and commitment to achieve company objectives, as well as those of your own organizational unit.

LEADERSHIP VERSUS MANAGEMENT

To understand leadership, it is important to grasp the difference between leadership and management. We get a clue from the standard way of framing the functions of management: planning, organizing, leading, and controlling. Leading is a major part of a manager's job, yet a manager must also plan, organize, and control.

Leadership also deals with change, inspiration, motivation, and influence, while management deals more with maintaining equilibrium. Here are some more points of differentiation between leadership and management:

- Management is more formal and scientific than leadership. It relies on foundation skills such as planning, budget control, and making effective use of information technology.

- Management uses an explicit set of tools and techniques, based on reasoning and testing, that you can apply in a variety of situations. Leadership has fewer explicit tools.

- Leadership involves having a vision of what the organization or organizational unit can become. The role of management is to implement the vision.

- Leadership requires eliciting teamwork and cooperation from a large network of people and motivating a substantial number of people in that network. Management is less concerned about motivating a large network of people.

- A leader frequently displays enthusiasm, passion, and inspiration to get others to attain high levels of performance. Managing involves less emotion and more careful acting to achieve goals after they are defined.

- A leader makes frequent use of creative problem solving and imagination to bring about change. A manager tends toward making more frequent use of standard, well-established solutions to problems.

 Vision A vision is an idealized scenario of what the future of an organization or an organizational unit can become.

While it's important to appreciate the difference between leadership and management, don't go overboard. If the views expressed here are taken to the extreme, the leader becomes an inspirational figure and the manager becomes a plodding bureaucrat stuck in the status quo.

So don't downplay the importance of management. Effective leaders have to be good managers, or be supported by effective managers. Leadership is vital for the success of organizations and society, but management is also necessary for achieving good results.

Remember to Exercise Leadership   Suppose you are dutifully going about your job as a manager or staff professional; your results are satisfactory but your group is not achieving exceptional or exciting results. It's time to exercise leadership. You need to be passionate, persuasive, imaginative, and visionary.

LEADERSHIP AS A PARTNERSHIP

Another way of understanding leadership is that it is a partnership between the leader and group members. The term partnership reflects the relatively equal power between the leader and his or her constituents. Leaders who are partners of group members welcome their input on major decisions.

The leader can still provide direction and inspiration while regarding group members as partners rather than employees or subordinates. For a valid partnership to exist, the following conditions must be met:

- The leader develops a vision only after receiving input from his or her partners.

- Group members have the right to disagree with the leader because they are regarded as valuable contributors to the group effort.

- Both the leader and the group members are held accountable for results. If the group members want to be treated as partners, they also have to risk being accountable for accomplishments as well as failures.

- Both the leader and the group members are honest with each other. Not telling the truth is a violation of the implied contract between the leader and the group members.

In this lesson you learned about the meaning of leadership, how leadership contrasts with management, and why to think of leadership as a partnership between the leader and group members.

2

How to Develop Positive Self-Talk

In this lesson you will learn that by developing positive self-talk you will increase your self-confidence. Self-confidence is an important characteristic of leaders because it inspires confidence in others.

The Seven Steps of Positive Self-Talk

To appear self-confident and to project a strong leadership image, positive self-talk must replace negative self-talk. Positive self-talk involves saying positive things about oneself to oneself. Positive self-talkers also make positive statements about themselves when speaking to others. When asked by his manager if he can take on a difficult assignment, the positive self-talker would say something to the effect: "Let me give it a shot. My track record in dealing with the near-impossible has been good so far."

The biggest leadership dividends from positive self-talk come when positive self-talk takes place in front of others. The seven steps in positive self-talk require careful concentration to understand. In addition, self-discipline is needed to implement the seven steps successfully.

1. Objectively state the incident that is creating doubt about your capabilities. The key word here is "objectively." Terry, who is fearful of poorly executing a customer satisfaction survey for the company might say: "I've been asked to conduct a customer satisfaction survey for the company, and I'm not good at conducting surveys."

2. Objectively interpret what the incident does not mean. Terry might say, "Not being skilled at conducting a survey doesn't mean that I can't figure out a way to do a useful survey, or that I'm an ineffective employee."

3. Objectively state what the incident does mean. To implement this step, the person should avoid putdown labels such as "incompetent," "stupid," "dumb," "jerk," or "airhead." All these terms are forms of negative self-talk. Terry should state what the incident does mean: "I have a problem with one small aspect of this job—conducting a customer survey. This means I need to acquire skill in conducting a survey."

4. Objectively account for the cause of the incident. Terry could say, "I'm really worried about conducting an accurate survey because I have very little experience of this nature."

5. Identify some positive ways to prevent the incident from happening again. Terry might say, "I'll buy a book on conducting surveys and follow it carefully," or "I'll enroll in a seminar on conducting customer surveys."

6. Use positive self-talk. Terry imagines the boss saying, "This survey is really good. I'm proud of my decision to select you to conduct this important survey."

When the opportunity arises Terry will say to the boss: "I'm glad you asked me to conduct the survey. I'm eager to take on new challenges, and I've done well with them in the past." Or, Terry might say to the boss, "Thanks for the opportunity for professional growth."

7. Keep the momentum going by starting each day with positive thoughts. Positive self-talk is a complex habit that requires frequent reinforcement and reinvigoration. Invest at least five minutes each day to create constructive energy. Just before launching the day's activities is a good time for most people.

Find a quiet place free from interruptions, get comfortable, breathe deeply, and think positive thoughts. Tell yourself that you can meet any professional or personal challenges that life has to offer. Think about your recent positive accomplishments and all the compliments you have received in the last thirty days.

 List Your Personal Assets To quickly rejuvenate your positive self-talk habit, list your seven most positive personal assets. A personal asset in this context refers to an individual quality rather than a financial or tangible asset. A sample list might read: "Above-average intelligence, great people skills, a whiz at information technology, great ethics, a winning smile, excellent job experience, and boundless energy."

Positive self-talk builds self-confidence because it programs the mind with positive messages. Making frequent positive messages or affirmations about the self creates a more confident person and projects a more positive image. An example would be, "I know I can learn this new software rapidly enough to increase my productivity within five days." If you do make a mistake, the right positive self-talk (to yourself or in front of others) might be: "It's taken me more time than usual to learn how to use this new software, but I know I'll have the problem licked in a few days."

Avoiding Negative Self-Talk

As previously mentioned, to boost self-confidence you should minimize negative statements about yourself and therefore appear more like a leader. A lack of self-confidence is reflected in such statements as,

> "I may be stupid but ..."

> "Nobody asked my opinion."

> "I know I'm usually wrong, but ..."

> "I know I don't have as much education as some people, but ..."

Self-effacing statements like these serve to reinforce low self-confidence. Instead, look on your weak points as areas for possible self-improvement. Negative self-labeling can do long-term damage to your self-confidence and leadership ability.

Reprogramming the Brain to Achieve Positive Self-talk

Positive self-talking may involve changing the mental set, attitude, or belief that supports the outcome you want to change. To reprogram your brain to prepare yourself for becoming a positive self-talker, try the system developed at the Center for Management Effectiveness in Pacific Palisades, California. Use this system in conjunction with the seven-step approach described previously. The two systems supplement each other. You will particularly need the system described next if you're not making rapid enough progress using the first system. The system for reprogramming the brain consists of five steps:

1. Decide specifically what you want to do to better increase your effectiveness, satisfaction, or growth. In this instance, you want to become a positive self-talker.

2. Affirm that the desired behavior is already happening. Use the *present* tense. "If you say, I *will* become a positive self-talker and project a leader-type image," the result is placed in the future where it may remain beyond your immediate grasp. Instead, use the positive self-affirmation, "I *am* a positive self-talker who projects self-confidence."

3. Include your feelings as part of your affirmation. You might say, "I'm thrilled about being able to say so many positive things about myself, and not having to put myself down so often."

4. Affirm the positive. Instead of saying, "I'm no longer going to make those put-down statements about myself," say, "I *am* a positive self-talker. Each day I think positively about myself."

5. Affirm only what you truly believe is possible. Positive self-affirmations work best with accomplishments that your natural talents and acquired skills will allow. In this case, you might affirm that you will greatly increase the ratio of positive self-talk to negative self-talk.

When you implement your program of self-affirmations it is important to write down your affirmations and review them at least twice each week. Stay with the weekly reviews until you achieve the intended results. Also, remember to imagine what it will be like to have achieved your goal of positive self-talk. Visualize yourself making so many positive statements about yourself that others believe in your self-confidence. At the same time they will perceive you to be a leader.

Be Self-Effacing on Occasion   Suppose you have mastered the art of self-talk, and you begin to get vibes that you are irritating others with your image of perfection. Throw in an occasional self-effacing comment just to humanize yourself. You might say, "My twelve-year old told me he would teach me how to use my electronic camera real soon." Remember your goal is to increase the ratio of positive self-affirmations to negative ones, not to glow like an announcer on a home-shopping network!

In this lesson you learned about developing and using positive self-talk to increase your self-confidence and become a more effective leader.

3

HOW TO USE POSITIVE VISUAL IMAGERY

In this lesson you will learn how to use the powerful force of visual imagery to strengthen your self-confidence and leadership impact.

HOW VISUAL IMAGERY WORKS

Leaders have to appear confident and in control in most work situations. An example would be a meeting with a member of upper-management who is prepared to swing the budget ax. Your intuitive reaction is that if you cannot handle his concerns about the size of your department's budget, your budget will be drastically reduced. An important technique in handling this situation is positive visual imagery. It requires you to picture a positive outcome in your mind.

APPLYING VISUAL IMAGERY

To apply positive visual imagery, imagine yourself engaging in a convincing argument about retaining your present budget for the next fiscal year. Imagine talking in positive terms about the excellent return on investment your department provides the organization. Imagine yourself explaining in a convincing fashion that your department is an *investment* for the company, not a *cost*.

Visualize yourself listening patiently to the executive's concerns about spending too much money next year. Imagine yourself agreeing sympathetically with the idea that every dollar spent by the company should contribute to profit. Rehearse in your mind explaining to the executive that your department has already eliminated processes that don't add value for the customer.

As you rehearse this scenario in your mind, create a mental picture of you and the executive shaking hands in agreement that your budget will be retained at its current level for the next fiscal year. Or, if you are feeling a little less bold, imagine escaping with only a ten-percent budget reduction. Visualization is not designed to perform miracles.

 Positive Visual Imagery   Positive visual imagery is picturing a positive outcome in your mind of a situation facing you right now or in the future.

What Visual Imagery Does for You

Positive visual imagery helps you appear self-confident because your mental rehearsal of the situation has helped you prepare for battle. You are less anxious about situations for which you are well prepared.

If positive visual imagery works for you once, you will be even more effective in future situations. For example, next week you might need to visualize how you, as a leader, will resolve conflict between two bickering team members.

SUGGESTIONS FOR USING VISUAL IMAGERY

Applying positive visual imagery is straightforward. Imagine yourself engaging in a behavior that will accomplish what you want. Visualization is widely used by sports trainers and sports psychologists to help athletes achieve specific performance targets.

Coaches often teach basketball players to picture a foul shot going through the net without hitting the rim or the backboard. Tennis players visualize their serve landing at a specific point in the receiver's court. The following suggestions will elevate your visualization skills:

- Before you begin visualization, relax and get comfortable.

- Think only about the immediate challenge you are facing. Visualization won't work when several topics compete for your attention.

- Concentrate intently. Concentration and visualization go hand in hand. Concentration is a major contributor to high performance.

- Relax the best you can even if you are visualizing a stressful situation. Visualization was originally developed by psychiatrists to help their patients prepare for anxiety-provoking situations.

- Create an imaginary videotape of yourself in action, speaking and acting in a self-confident, composed manner. Imagine your facial expressions, your hand movements, and how you are moving your body.

- Practice reproducing an aroma in your mind, such as freshly baked bread or the perfume of somebody special in your life. The purpose of this exercise is to bring visualization to a high level.

- Use multiple senses as part of your visualization. Imagine the touch of people shaking your hands, the aroma of your new office furniture, and the sight of the smile on your face.

Pause for Ten Seconds At times you will need positive visual imagery to get you through an un-anticipated challenge, such as suddenly being called into a meeting to defend an action you took. Although you are pressed for time, pause for ten seconds, close your eyes, and imagine a positive outcome. A quick visualization may not be perfect but it should give you the boost in self-confidence you need to defend your actions admirably.

Using Positive Visual Imagery to Overcome Adversity

The ability to overcome adversity is an outstanding leadership behavior. Visualization can help you overcome adversity. Imagine yourself enjoying a successful outcome to an adverse circumstance you are facing. Wishing alone won't make it happen, but visualizing a positive conclusion will prompt you to use all your creative energy to make it come true. In addition, consider these specific suggestions:

- Specify in your mind what "overcoming adversity" means. Does it mean you make a big enough sale to finally catch up with your quota? Does it mean finding the type of job you want at the type of company that would match your personality?

- Make your visualization as specific as possible. Imagine what it would feel like to be back on a full-time payroll, or to be promoted to your former organizational level.

- Include multiple components in your visualization. Develop several different images that would be part of your victory package. The images might include being hugged by your loved ones for having overcome a setback, or being congratulated by associates for having found meaningful work for the group.

Keep Practicing Visualization   You've followed the instructions carefully in this lesson, so you feel ready to visualize your way out of any challenge facing you. One day you perform poorly during a moment of truth even though you had a clear visualization of success in that situation. Don't give up yet. Visualization will only contribute to your success when other success factors are in place, such as having the right information and problem-solving skills to deal with the situation. Keep practicing visualization, and keep preparing yourself for challenges in other ways.

In this lesson you learned how to use positive visual imagery to enhance your self-confidence and leadership stature in a variety of situations. You also learned how to use positive visual imagery to help you overcome adversity.

4

How to Exhibit Personal Dynamism

In this lesson you will learn how to project personal dynamism and self-confidence, both important for having others perceive you as a leader.

An especially effective way of appearing self-confident is to be perceived as dynamic, or filled with energy and vitality. If you are naturally energetic and outgoing, just be yourself. The energy you display already contributes to the perception of you as being in control and a leader. When this happens you will find that you will naturally become more self-confident and appear more like a leader. If your personality is subdued, you can still develop behaviors that will make you appear dynamic. Six behaviors are reviewed in this chapter.

Personal Dynamism Personal dynamism is a special quality about a person that makes him or her appear filled with energy, vitality, and self-confidence, like a leader. Such dynamism inspires self-confidence in others as well.

EXPRESSING YOUR FEELINGS ASSERTIVELY

One tactic for appearing more dynamic is to express your feelings in an open, constructive, and candid manner. Visualize the scenario of a staff meeting, for example, in which the participants are weighing the pros and cons of a proposal. Most people make factual statements such as, "I see some merit in this idea. It could be cost-effective in the short range," or "This proposal has a lot of weaknesses. I doubt it will bring about a suitable return on the investment."

In contrast to these emotionally neutral statements, a dynamic person will project feelings about the proposals. Feeling statements move people, and that is a leader's role. To exhibit personal dynamism, make a statement such as, "Your proposed solution really excites [great feeling word] me. The idea would pay for itself in no time, and we would all be very proud [another great feeling word]."

On the other hand, if you disliked the proposal, you might state, "This proposal has a lot of weaknesses that really worry [a strong feeling word] me. It will most likely backfire [a word that provokes feelings in others], and lose money [an explicitly bad state of affairs]."

USING ANIMATED FACIAL EXPRESSIONS

It is essential to frequently use animated facial expressions to exhibit personal dynamism. Use big smiles, little smiles, expressions of delight, frowns, scowls, looks of puzzlement, surprise, and reassuring nods. Remember that animated facial expressions project leadership characteristics. They show you are listening and involved.

To develop your skill at using animated facial expressions to help communicate your feelings, follow these suggestions:

- Pay attention to leaders you admire and note their facial expressions and model their behavior.

- Practice in front of a mirror or camcorder. Videotaping is better than a mirror because many people find it difficult to modify their facial expressions when looking into a mirror.

- While looking into the mirror or recording on tape, think of various moods you want to project, and then do your best to match your facial expression to the mood.

- If you need some guidelines for matching facial expressions to your mood, emulate television actors, newscasters, newsmakers, and especially comedians.

TALKING WITH OPTIMISM

Optimistic people, almost by definition, project an image of self-confidence and dynamism. You don't have to overhaul your personality if you are naturally pessimistic. Nevertheless, you can learn to keep some of your pessimistic thoughts to yourself and search for optimistic comments to fit each situation. Try these ideas for starters:

- When you have struggled through a rough assignment and finally completed it, talk about how you have benefited from the experience and will do even better next time.

- When you have barely met your quota, do not apologize. Talk positively about how you overcame unforeseen hurdles and squeaked through to accomplish your goals.

Projecting Optimism An important means of projecting optimism is to look for the positives in what other people perceive to be a negative event. For example, visualize yourself as a sales manager and sales plunged to a ten-year low. Instead of complaining and looking for excuses, say: "We have finally hit bottom. From now on we can expect an upturn. My plans for a turnaround will be completed by next Monday."

LOOKING AND ACTING POWERFUL

An indispensable part of projecting personal dynamism is to look and act powerful. Looking powerful is more subtle than would appear on the surface. If you take literally the advice of wardrobe consultants, you will look like a sales associate in a posh retail store or like a young professional in most metropolitan offices.

On the other hand, if you ignore conventional wisdom about looking powerful you risk looking unimportant and lacking dynamism. Specific ways of increasing your power-look include:

- Dress with taste and style. Suits for men and women should be conservative, but not too conservative. Your shirts may have initialed cuffs. Consider using an expensive fountain pen and watch. Women may consider adding a scarf to their outfit. If casual clothing is the norm, wear carefully pressed pants or slacks, starched, open-collar button-down shirts, and a sport coat.

- Decorate your office or cubicle tastefully, perhaps with stainless steel, leather, and polished glass. Use family photos and other mementos sparingly.

- On occasion, when standing, place hands on hips and place your feet apart about 18 inches. (Try it—it projects self-confidence.)

- For emphasis when speaking, point the index finger parallel to the ground, and thumb at a right angle— similar to aiming a water pistol (but do this only if you feel comfortable doing so).

Moving and Acting Purposefully

People who stride through the workplace as if they have an urgent purpose in mind project personal dynamism. Top-level managers move and act purposefully even when they are passing through a lobby. Keep these examples in mind:

- You arrive early for a meeting. Don't stand outside the room waiting for others to arrive; it makes you look like you're wasting time. Instead, take a seat in the meeting room and either read your memos or work on your To Do list.

- You are walking down the hallway to attend a meeting—stop to chat only if it meets some business purpose. Otherwise, walk in a straight line at a brisk pace.

Using a Firm Handshake

It should come as no surprise that a a firm handshake continues to be perceived by many people as a key indicator of self-confidence and dynamism. If your handshake is limp, make a point to tighten your grip. On the other hand, don't squeeze so hard as to hurt the other person. Both a limp and a too-tight handshake draw negative attention.

You Can't Be Dynamic to Everybody   Despite your best efforts, some people will not perceive you as having personal dynamism. The purpose of this lesson is to increase the percentage of people who will regard you as self-confident. Don't waste your time attempting to impress everybody—it's an impossible task.

Projecting Personal Dynamism Doesn't Happen Overnight   Suppose you have already tried out a few of the ideas in this section and you still do not feel that you are projecting enough personal dynamism. Not to worry! Projecting personal dynamism and self-confidence as a natural part of your behavior takes time. Just keep at it, and soon enough you will see the results in how others respond to you.

In this lesson you learned about how to project personal dynamism and self-confidence and learned key behaviors that will help you do this.

Using Nonverbal Communication in Leading

In this lesson you will learn how to use nonverbal communication to project an image of leadership and self-confidence.

Nonverbal Ways to Project Confidence and Leadership

You're probably familiar with different ways of communicating nonverbally, such as gestures, posture, and eye movements. There are certain gestures that say to others you are self-confident and a leader. Not everybody interprets body language and other nonverbal signals uniformly. Yet, using the types of nonverbal communication described in this lesson will impress many, but not all, of the people you want to influence.

Nonverbal Communication Nonverbal communication is the transmission of messages through means other than words.

HEAD, FACE, AND EYE MOVEMENTS

When used in combination, the head, face, and eyes provide the clearest indication of attitudes toward other people. When addressing another a person, moving your head, face, and eyes toward that individual and giving them your full attention suggests self-confidence. When you have good eye contact with the person you're talking to, that individual will interpret more favorably what you have to say than messages sent without eye contact. And if you maintain eye contact with group members, they will pay more attention to you and perceive you as more confident.

POSTURE

Posture is perhaps the most obvious nonverbal signal of self-confidence and leadership ability. Standing up straight generally reflects high self-confidence, while stooping and slouching means a poor self-image. Leaning toward other individuals suggests that you are favorably disposed toward them and what they have to say.

BODY POSITION AND INTERPERSONAL DISTANCE

How far you stand from people you are attempting to influence and lead can shape their perceptions of your confidence as a leader? If you are in actual physical contact with a person or up to about 18 inches away this might be interpreted as confidence and brashness. But you might also be perceived as intimidating or harassing.

Standing from about one and one-half to four feet from the person you're talking to is best for projecting face-to-face leadership.

If you move from about four to eight feet away from the person you're addressing, you might appear to be shying away from others.

HAND GESTURES

Hand gestures provide an opportunity to project confidence and an in-charge attitude. Consider these possibilities:

- Punching a fist into the air to mean "Let's do it!"

- Using a finger as a pointing rod to emphasize a point or direct others.

- Open-palm slapping of another's hand to signify strong agreement or to offer congratulations.

- Both palms extended in the same motion required for pushing a heavy object, will communicate forcefully the message, "I don't want to hear any more of this."

- Extending a thumb upward indicating strong approval.

- The politician-like two arms raised in a V-shape with the first two fingers of each hand also in a V-shape is a high-power leadership gesture of unity and victory.

VOICE QUALITY AND TONE

People often attach more significance to the way you say something than to what you say. A forceful voice, which includes a consistent tone without vocalized pauses, suggests power, control, and confidence. A whispery, wimpy voice detracts from a person sounding confident and being able to take charge. A voice coach surveyed 1,000 men and women, and asked,

"Which irritating or unpleasant voice annoys you the most?"
The answer was a whining, complaining, or nagging tone. To
improve your voice quality, try these techniques:

- Listen to your recorded voice. Keep repeating the
  same message until you are satisfied that you sound
  like a confident person.

- Several times per week, visualize yourself speaking to
  group members, and practice using the voice quality
  you think will convey confident leadership.

PERSONAL APPEARANCE

Your external image plays an important role in communicating messages to others. People pay more respect and grant
more privileges to those they perceive as being well-dressed
and neatly groomed. Even on dress-down days, the majority of
effective leaders will choose clothing that gives them a professional look. Appearance includes more than the choice of
clothing. Self-confidence is projected by such small items as:

- Neatly pressed, clean clothing and polished shoes

- Impeccable fingernails and well-maintained hair

- Clean jewelry in mint condition

- Clean, white teeth

- A trace of cologne, perfume, or toilet water

USE OF TIME

A subtle form of nonverbal communication in the workplace
is the use of time. Guarding time as a precious resource will
help you project self-confidence and leadership. A statement such as, "I can give 15 minutes to your problem this

Wednesday at 4 p.m." says to another that you are in control of yourself. (Too many of these statements, however, might make you appear unapproachable and lacking consideration.) Suggestions for projecting self-confidence and leadership behavior through the use of time include:

- Being prompt for meetings and starting and stopping meetings on time if you are the leader

- Jotting down appointments in your day planner or electronic device in front of others

- Making references to dates one year into the future and beyond, such as "By 2001 we should have a 35 percent market share."

HOW TO APPEAR CONFIDENT, FRIENDLY, AND APPROACHABLE

Another important use of body language is to present a confident, but friendly image to others in the workplace. Such behavior is typical of the team, or participative, style of leader. Consider these nonverbal ways to to indicate you are a team player:

- **Tie.** A loosened tie and slightly exposed throat can portray openness and informality.

- **Toes.** Dominant people tend to stand with their toes pointing outward, while less dominant people point their toes slightly inward.

- **Shoulders.** Shrugged or rounded shoulders make you appear less threatening. Taking off a jacket with padded shoulders can make you appear less distant.

- **Hands.** Placing your forearms on the table, palms up, will make your words seem more sincere. If you disagree with your boss, open your palms to send out the subliminal message that you defer to his or her authority even while disagreeing.

- **Body.** Matching your body movements to those of the person you are communicating with (called mirroring) without being too obvious, creates a sense of solidarity that conveys a feeling of agreement with the other person.

Mirroring   Mirroring is copying the behavior of another. For example, if the person you're talking with folds her arms, you fold them as well. If the person crosses her legs, then you do it, too. Mirroring subtly tells others you want to have rapport with them.

Relax When Communicating with Others   The quickest way to improve your nonverbal communication is to relax when communicating with others. Take a deep breath and consciously allow your body muscles to loosen. A relaxed person makes it easier for other people to relax, and you will appear more confident and calm.

Nonverbal Signals that Detract From a Leadership Image

Part of communicating confidence through nonverbal behavior is to avoid negative signals that detract from your image.

A sampling of these negative behaviors is as follows:

- Nodding or smiling almost incessantly. Such behaviors make one appear insincere and insecure.

- Yawning. A yawner looks bored, fatigued, burned out, or a combination of all three.

- Playing with your hair, scratching your head, cracking your knuckles, or twiddling your thumbs. Enough said.

- In an era of hypersensitivity to sexual harassment, any touching beyond a handshake is questionable.

Use Multiple Nonverbal Signals   You've tried out several specific nonverbal communication signals on one or two people, and you didn't get the response you wanted. Keep trying. Recognize that a given nonverbal signal (such as punching your fist into the air) will influence some people but not others.

In this lesson you learned how to use nonverbal communication to project an image of leadership and self-confidence.

How to Use Visioning

In this lesson you will learn how to create and implement visions that will inspire and motivate group members.

Creating a Vision

Before working on a vision, it's important to dispel two widely circulated misunderstandings about visions. The first is that creating a vision is a full-time job. Top executives often say that their job is creating a vision for the organization, yet in reality they spend about 99 percent of the time engaged in other activities. Creating a vision is a high-impact activity, but it's not a full-time job.

The second misunderstanding is that visions are created only at the top of the organization. Effective leaders at every organizational level create vision statements.

Understanding the Nature of a Vision

Lesson 1 defined a vision as an idealized scenario of what the future of an organization or an organizational unit can become. To form a vision you have to look beyond the immediate future to create an image of what the organization or unit is capable of becoming.

A vision highlights the discrepancy between present and ideal conditions and provides people with something to strive toward. Being able to articulate a vision is another important characteristic of a leader.

Gathering Information for the Vision

A common assumption is that an effective leader is supposed to be a visionary possessing a storehouse of fabulous ideas. Yet the leader's own imagination is just one source of ideas for formulating a vision. There are many sources from which you can gather information to create a vision:

- Your own intuition about developments in your field, the markets you serve, and the preferences of your constituents.

- The work of futurists (specialists in making predictions about the future) as it relates to your type of work.

- Group discussion of what it would take to please the people your group serves.

- Annual reports and management books that describe the vision statements being formulated by others.

- Speaking to group members individually and collectively to learn of their hopes and dreams for the future.

- For an organizational unit, studying the entire organization's vision and developing one that is compatible.

Building a Vision or Mission Statement for the Group

Several consulting firms have developed a procedure for building a team mission statement that can also be used to build a vision statement for the group. "Missions" and "visions" have different technical definitions but in practice they overlap. A mission deals more specifically with the purpose of the unit or organization and where it fits into the world. A vision is a loftier image of the future.

Building a vision or mission statement for the group consists of four steps:

1. Clarify customer requirements. What do your internal or external customers want?

Internal Customers   Internal customers are those other employees whose work depends on what you do. For example, the internal customers for the accounting staff are executives who depend on the data the accounting staff provides to make sound business decisions.

2. List the group or firm's distinctive competencies compared to others, that is, what it is better at than anyone else. Such internal analysis can be supplemented by asking a few internal and external customers what they think are your group or firm's distinctive competencies.

3. Have each individual write a vision or mission statement that meets the criteria for an effective one. The statement should provide energy and excitement, be concise, and easily remembered.

4. Create and reach consensus on a vision or mission statement. Contrary to widespread practice, the preparation of vision and mission statements does not require several lengthy retreats. Three hours is ample time to complete the mission statement after you've collected data about customer requirements.

For the vision or mission statement to be effective, group members must identify with it. Vision and mission statements have an uplifting quality and point toward a new standard of excellence.

Reinforcing Mission and Vision Statements   A big challenge the leader faces is to keep the vision or mission statement on the minds of group members. Some companies have the statement printed on plastic cards that fit readily into wallets, on small plaques attached to key rings, or on beverage mugs.

CHARACTERISTICS OF AN EFFECTIVE VISION STATEMENT

Given that a vision statement is supposed to inspire people by giving them a broader purpose than their immediate jobs, it should be powerful. Keep these characteristics in mind in formulating a vision statement. It should:

- Provide energy, excitement, and direction
- Be simple and concise, usually 25 words or less
- Be easily remembered
- Represent an improvement over the current realities
- Be linked to organization strategy
- Be linked to the needs of customers, or any other public served
- Be a reflection of group values and aspirations
- Create a positive picture of the future for the work group
- Transcend the nuts and bolts of daily activities

- Be uplifting, but not so preposterously wonderful that it is viewed impossible to achieve

- Not so broad and general that it could fit almost any organization in any field

At this point you are probably saying to yourself, "What vision or mission statement could conceivably meet all those criteria?" Here are several vision and mission statements that appear to be doing the job:

- **CNN**: "To create the first truly global information company, the global network of record, seen in every nation on the planet, and broadcast in most major languages."

- **Chrysler Corporation**: "Chrysler Corporation is committed to providing our customers with the world's highest level of satisfaction with our products and services."

- **A facilities group at Raychem Corporation that fixes toilets and air conditioners**: "To make people feel good, to lift people's spirits through beauty, cleanliness, functionality, enthusiasm, good cheer, and excellence."

- **Fico's Automotive Repair & Refinish Collision**: "We intend to be the premier body shop for high-quality auto and small-truck restoration, refinishing, or body repair. We will be highly respected by auto buffs and insurance companies."

IMPLEMENTING THE VISION

Many experts contend that implementing a vision is the heart of managerial work. How to implement a vision is therefore as complex as the process of management. With this disclaimer in mind, here are several suggestions that deal specifically with implementing a vision or mission:

- Remind people often of the vision or mission.

- Frequently mention the fact that if the vision is implemented correctly, there will be more rewards, recognition, and excitement for all workers.

- Measure progress toward the vision periodically. If your intent is to become a world-class provider of goods or services in your field, have your customer satisfaction ratings improved recently?

- Develop a sense of ownership in the vision by asking those who helped formulate it how well they are doing.

- Relate organizational visions to personal visions. Ask people to submit in writing how the vision of the organization or unit fits in with their career aspirations.

- Modify the vision or mission as circumstances change to keep it vibrant and useful.

Fine-Tune Your Mission or Vision Statement
You and your group have crafted a vision or mission statement that you think is awesome. Yet, six months later, neither performance nor behavior has changed. Your vision or mission statement might need fine-tuning to make it more company-specific. Most vision and mission statements contain the same generalities about satisfying customers, providing high quality, and becoming world class. They are often too generalized and idealistic to be motivational.

In this lesson you learned how to create and implement visions that will inspire and motivate group members.

LESSON

7

How to Develop a Masterful Communication Style

In this lesson you will learn how to develop and implement a communication style that will inspire and motivate group members.

Expressing Optimism

Being a masterful communicator means more than knowing the mechanics of good speech and grammar. No matter how articulate you are, being grumpy will limit your inspirational appeal. Even if you are a natural pessimist, you can learn to express optimism in the presence of group members. A few suggestions for the aspiring optimist are as follows:

- Frame even negative messages in positive terms. Suppose you are a retail store executive and you discover that your turnover rate is 40 percent per year. Your analysis is that such high turnover is too costly and creates customer service problems. You tell your store managers, "If we can cut our turnover rate by just 10 percent we will be beat the industry average, reduce costs, and improve customer satisfaction."

- Phrase scenarios in terms of what can be done or what will be done. Similar to the suggestion just made, tell people how conditions can be or will be improved.

- Provide a clear-cut course of action.

- Substitute positive terms for negative ones when feasible. Examples include "challenge" for "problem," "major investment" for "major cost," "developmental opportunity" for "personal weakness," and "best suited for yesterday's challenges" for "obsolete."

Using Heavy-Impact, Embellishing Language

Certain words used in the proper context give power and force to your speech. Used naturally and sincerely, these words can strengthen your leadership stature and your ability to inspire others. Current buzzwords usually have an impact. Note the emphasis on *current*. Yesterday's buzzwords have low-impact. Here is is a sampling of heavy-impact, embellishing language:

- Tell group members that you want them to "unleash their creative potential" instead of simply asking that they make a few suggestions.

- Talk about having attended a "prestigious" trade show rather than simply a trade show.

- Use the term "on the verge" of accomplishing something as long as a project is in process.

- Mention that you want the group to "bond" with customers instead of simply stating that you want them to establish a good working relationship.

- Ask the team to "do it right the first time" instead of simply avoiding mistakes.

- When your department has won an interdepartmental skirmish, or won a bid over a competitor, mention that you have "nuked" them.

Using heavy-impact, embellishing language is an important addition to your leadership tool kit. Yet if embellishment is taken too far, too often, the embellisher might appear deceptive and devious.

INSPIRING OTHERS WITH ANALOGIES AND METAPHORS

A well-chosen analogy or metaphor appeals to the intellect, imagination, and values. Effective leaders therefore make frequent use of analogies and metaphors. An analogy draws attention to the similarity between the features of two things, so people can make a comparison. Workers are excited and inspired by analogies that are relevant to the challenges they face. Here is a sampling of analogies leaders have used in their interactions with group members:

- We are a young company competing against the established giants, much like Compaq Computer of 15 years ago.

- As financial planners, we provide a service to our clients as important as the help they receive from their accountants and lawyers.

- Don't be discouraged by placing second in our bid to receive that contract. Michael Jordan didn't make his high-school basketball team on the first try.

A metaphor is also a comparison, but the comparison is between two objects not ordinarily associated with each other. A new-product manager might state, "Don't let those comments about our new model being mundane discourage you. Look at the bum rap people give donkeys. Yet donkey-owners love their hard-working, faithful animals. A donkey can be counted on for years of good performance. Besides that a donkey-owner will form an emotional attachment to his or her unglamorous sidekick."

Using Anecdotes

Another aspect of the communication style of effective leaders is that they make extensive use of memorable anecdotes to get messages across. They inspire and instruct team members by telling fascinating stories. Using anecdotes is a powerful leadership technique for several reasons:

- People like to hear anecdotes.

- Anecdotes help build the corporate culture.

- Workers can remember a principle or policy better if it is accompanied by an anecdote.

Management by Anecdote   Management by anecdotes is the technique of inspiring and instructing team members by telling fascinating stories.

Message-ending anecdotes might relate to such subjects as a company president going out of his way to help an individual customer, or a lower-ranking employee who defied authority to meet her job responsibilities. In the latter instance, a receptionist at IBM denied admission to the company chairman, Tom Watson because he was not wearing a security badge. Instead of firing the young woman, Watson praised her devotion to duty.

Create an Anecdote File   Anecdote telling is such a useful management and leadership technique that it merits special attention. Create a useful anecdote file of your own. Collect anecdotes you observe personally, those you hear from others, and those you read in books, magazines, and newsletters.

RELY HEAVILY ON NONVERBAL COMMUNICATION

Lesson 5 described how to use nonverbal communication to enhance your self-confidence and strengthen your leadership impact. Nonverbal communication is also an essential ingredient of masterful communication. Keep these points in mind:

- Nonverbal communication provides the emphasis and believability to the message itself.

- The right nonverbal signals can prevent you from appearing like a cold fish in spite of the emotion-provoking words you choose.

- Nonverbal signals help communicate the emotional content to your message.

MINIMIZING JUNK WORDS AND VOCALIZED PAUSES

Using colorful, powerful words enhances the perception by others that you are a leader. It is also important to minimize the use of words and phrases that dilute the impact of your speech. Such junk words and vocalized pauses convey the impression that you do not have the self-assurance and intelligence required of a leader—especially in a professional setting. Frequently used junk words and vocalized pauses include:

- Like (used invariably before almost any expression)
- You know (to start almost any sentence)
- You know what I'm saying?
- He goes (to mean he says)
- Uhhhhhh
- Frequent clearing of the throat for no physical reason

An effective way of decreasing the use of these extraneous words and nonwords is to tape your side of a phone conversation and then play it back. Once you hear how these junk words and vocalized pauses detract from your speech effectiveness, you can monitor your own speech for improvement.

SUPPORTING CONCLUSIONS WITH DATA

You will have more leadership stature if you back your spoken presentations with solid data. Convincing data for your arguments can also be obtained from published sources including online services or collected by you. Keep these points in mind:

- Be specific about the source of your data rather than say, "Research shows that...."

- When possible, use reliable, prestigious sources. Surveys conducted by *Business Week* will impress more people than those by *The National Enquirer*!

- Avoid glib statements such as "Economists agree that...." or "Psychologists agree that...." Economists and psychologists have substantial differences of opinions among themselves.

- Do not rely on research so much that you appear to
  have no faith in your own intuition.

 Rework Your Material   You are attempting to
strengthen the impact of your communication
style, yet in one or two situations your presentation
fails to excite group members. Rework your material, and try again. Sometimes an expression or
anecdote that you think is powerful is just not a
good fit for your constituents.

In this lesson you learned how to develop and use a masterful
communication style.

8

How to Be a Transformational Leader

In this lesson you will learn what it takes to become a transformational leader, including the specific tasks carried out by such leaders.

Characteristics and Qualities of Transformational Leaders

The most influential leaders in the workplace are those who can transform the firm from poor to outstanding performance.

Transformational leaders make sure their interactions with people go beyond just evaluating their performance and rewarding them for good performance. Rather, they lead companies and people to a high ground. Transformational leaders also help turn around troubled organizations, and guide them toward a state of health.

Transformational Leader A transformational leader is one who helps organizations and people make substantial positive changes in the way they do things.

CHARISMA

Transformational leaders usually possess charisma. They instill pride, faith, and respect. Transformational leaders have a gift for detecting what is really important to people and the organization, and they are able to transmit a sense of vision and mission. Charisma, in fact, is close in meaning to personal dynamism. Similar to personal dynamism, a person can't become charismatic in one week. Nevertheless, if the following list of actions are practiced regularly a person will be perceived as charismatic.

- **Use visioning**. If you are the leader of an organizational unit, develop a dream about its future. Discuss your vision with others in the unit, and with your immediate manager.

- **Make frequent use of metaphors.** Develop metaphors to inspire people around you.

- **Inspire trust and confidence.** Make your deeds consistent with your promises. Get people to believe in your competence by making your accomplishments known in a polite, tactful way.

- **Make others feel capable.** Give out assignments in which others can succeed, and lavishly praise their success.

- **Be highly energetic and goal oriented.** Impress others with your energy and resourcefulness. To increase your energy supply, exercise frequently, eat well, and get ample rest including power naps.

- **Express your emotions and feelings frequently.** Freely express warmth, joy, happiness, and enthusiasm.

- **Smile frequently, even if you're not in a happy mood**. A warm smile usually indicates a confident, caring person, which contributes to a perception of charisma.

- **Make everybody you meet feel that he or she is important**. At a company meeting, for example, make it a point to meet and shake the hand of everyone there.

tip

Remember People's Names   The quickest way to make people feel important is to remember their names and the nature of the project they are working on, particularly if you're not their immediate manager.

INSPIRATION TO OTHERS

Transformational leaders inspire group members to exceed their initial expectations. People are also inspired when they receive emotional support from the leader. Techniques of emotional support include:

- Making encouraging statements to a group member who isn't sure if he or she can execute a difficult assignment.

- Expressing sincere concern when a group member, or one of his or her loved-ones, is severely ill.

- Listening to group members talk about work or personal problems.

- Complimenting a group member for outstanding effort as well as outstanding results.

INDIVIDUALIZED ATTENTION TO PEOPLE

Another aspect of being a transformational leader is to engage in actions that reflect consideration for individuals. A transformational leader treats each group member as an individual and gives special attention to his or her concerns. For example, the transformational leader recognizing individual problems might work with an employee to develop a flexible work schedule to provide for the needs of a family member in poor health.

INTELLECTUAL STIMULATION TO PEOPLE

An intellectually stimulating leader encourages group members to look at old problems or methods in new ways. Techniques for providing intellectual stimulation include:

- Asking what-if questions such as, "What if a massive recession took place next year? How would we cope with it?"

- Asking group members how certain news events might affect the company.

- Asking the group to develop a plan for implementing a new management technique within the unit.

- Collaborating with group members in developing a business strategy for your product or service.

RISK TAKING

A leader with a risk-taking attitude is willing to take chances even in the midst of adversity. The transformational leader may appear to be a gambler, and be willing to risk the company to take it in a particular direction because he or she believes it will yield results worth the risk. Risk takers are also trustful of others which makes it easier for them to take risks.

INNOVATION

It is essential for transformational leaders to be innovative. They cannot rely on established methods and courses of action to cope with major challenges. Transformational leaders have a propensity for finding novel solutions to new and old problems.

HOW TRANSFORMATIONS TAKE PLACE

To be a transformational leader one must have the qualities and take the actions just described. Equally important is to understand how these qualities and actions move leaders to higher levels of accomplishment.

CHANGING THE ORGANIZATIONAL CULTURE

The most far-sweeping act of a transformational leader is to revamp the organizational culture. This means that the values, attitudes, and entire atmosphere of the organization change. The most typical change is to convert the culture from a low-risk taking, stiff bureaucratic one to a culture in which people are more adventuresome and less constrained by rules and regulations.

RAISING PEOPLE'S AWARENESS ABOUT REWARDS

The transformational leader makes group members aware of the importance and values of certain rewards and how to achieve them. He or she might point to the pride workers would experience should the firm become number one in its field. At the same time, the transformational leader should point to the financial rewards accompanying such success.

HELPING PEOPLE LOOK BEYOND SELF-INTEREST

The transformational leader helps group members look at the big picture for the good of the team and the organization. Bit by bit workers are made aware that their actions contribute to a broader purpose than satisfying their own interests. Here are some ways of helping people look beyond self-interest:

- The leader tells a group of supervisors and professionals, "I know some of you dislike word-processing your own letters and memos. But if we hire more administrative assistants, we will have to raise prices to a level at which we will be noncompetitive."

- The leader tells a group of haggard workers who have been putting in 65-hour weeks for two months. "I know you feel beaten into the ground. And you are upset and angry. Yet keep in mind that the project you are working on will revolutionize the field and you will be part of that revolution."

HELPING PEOPLE SEARCH FOR SELF-FULFILLMENT

The transformational leader helps people go beyond a focus on minor satisfactions to a quest for self-fulfillment. The leader might explain to a group of employees grumbling about the low-quality of food being served at a retreat, "I agree with you that the food being served here is disappointing. Yet, for a moment, think beyond the food. Every person here is being asked to participate in developing a new direction for the company. I suspect that is really more important to you than the food."

Helping People Understand the Need for Change

The transformational leader must help group members understand the need for change both emotionally and intellectually. The problem is that change involves dislocation and discomfort. A big change faced by many middle managers today is that they have to shift from the comforts of running a department, to being a team leader with much less authority. An effective transformational leader recognizes the emotional component to resisting change and deals with it openly. Ways of dealing with the emotions and attitudes surrounding change include:

- Conducting a one-on-one discussion about how the change might adversely affect the person

- Holding group discussions about the need for change in a competitive, changing environment

- Conducting a group discussion about the advantages and disadvantages of the change

- Presenting financial information about the need for change

Investing Others with a Sense of Urgency

To create the transformation, the leader assembles a critical mass of managers and other workers and involves them in a discussion about the urgency of change. The critical message must be communicated that "If we don't change now, there may be no future for our organization (or department)."

COMMITTING TO GREATNESS

The ultimate transformational act would be to get people excited about the prospects of doing great work and having a great organization. Everything else written in this book about leadership behavior would help contribute to greatness. Also, consider these suggestions:

- Have every worker write an essay about what would actually constitute greatness for the unit and the organization. Then hold a staff meeting about the key themes of the essays.

- Include a "greatness goal" in each worker's goal statement.

- Answer for yourself the question, "What would I have to do to feel like a great leader?"

In this lesson you learned how to become a transformational leader including the personal characteristics of a such a leader along with how transformations take place.

Establishing Your Power Base

In this lesson you will learn how to acquire some of the power you need to accomplish worthwhile goals for yourself and the organization.

Sources of Power for Yourself

Effective leaders are powerful people. They realize that a manager needs power to accomplish worthwhile goals.

> **Power** Power is the potential or ability to influence decisions and control resources.

An effective strategy for developing power is to recognize where power comes from in an organization, and then take steps to acquire some of that power.

LEGITIMATE POWER

Legitimate power can be obtained in only a few ways:

- Work hard to get promoted to a high-level position.
- Combine hard work with good connections to get promoted to a high-level position.
- Get the company to grant you more authority in your present position.
- Become a major stockholder in your company and demand a seat on the board of directors.
- Start your own company and build it into a substantial enterprise.

REWARD POWER

The authority to give employees rewards for compliance with directions and orders is reward power. If a vice president of manufacturing can directly reward supervisors with cash bonuses for achieving quality targets, the manager will exert considerable power. The more meaningful rewards you have at your disposal, the more reward power you can exert.

COERCIVE POWER

Coercive power means that a person is able to punish group members for noncompliance. Group members have to be somewhat dependent on the organization for coercive power to be effective. The leader who relies heavily on coercive power runs the constant threat of being ousted from power.

EXPERT POWER

A person who has talent, skill, and knowledge can exercise power. Expert power is the ability to influence others through specialized knowledge, skills, or abilities, like a marketing manager who is adept at identifying new markets. Suggestions for acquiring expert power include:

- Become a subject matter expert (SME) in an area that fits the present or future needs of the firm.

- Earn a degree or certificate in a technology or business strategy of interest to the firm.

- Identify an above-average skill of yours (such as negotiating good contracts) and develop the skill even further.

INFORMATION POWER

Information power stems from formal control over information that people need to do their work. A sales manager who controls the leads from customer inquiries holds considerable power. Information power can also stem from being in the know about key developments in the company or industry.

PRESTIGE POWER

Prestige power stems from one's status and reputation. A manager who has accumulated important business successes acquires prestige power. Executive recruiters (headhunters) are eager to keep on file the names of managers with prestige power.

Use Self-Promotion Prestige power takes a long time to develop, but you can sometimes hasten the process through self-promotion. Toot your own horn softly and let important people know of your accomplishments.

SOURCES OF POWER FOR YOUR UNIT

If you want to broaden your power base you must acquire power for your unit as well as for yourself. Sources of individual power apply somewhat to gaining power for your unit. For example, your department could acquire power because of its expertise.

POWER FROM PROVIDING RESOURCES

To stay in operation, organizations require a continuous flow of resources such as talented people, money, and technology. Units or departments in the organization that can provide the right resources acquire power.

POWER STEMMING FROM MANAGING CRITICAL PROBLEMS

Departments best able to cope with the firm's critical problems and uncertainties acquire relatively large amounts of power. For example, when a company faces complaints about quality, a group that can enhance quality will surge in power. To acquire the power that stems from managing critical problems, you as the manager would have to first spot critical problems. You'd then have to sell top management on your capability to solve those problems.

Power Stemming from Being Close to Power

An obvious fact of organizational life is that organizational units placed higher on the organization chart have more power than those at lower levels. What is not so obvious is that some leaders skillfully use office politics to get closer to power. Becoming liked by top-level managers, combined with good performance by your unit, is the best way of moving up the organization chart.

Tactics for Acquiring Power

Here are ten time-tested and ethical ways of acquiring power. Use the tactics that best fit your personal style and the circumstances you face.

- Develop power contacts. After powerful people have been identified, alliances with them must be established.

- Control vital information. Control generally refers to keeping the information covert until it serves one's purpose. Knowing how to maneuver contracts through private and governmental bureaucracies is an example of controlling vital information.

- Control lines of communication. Related to controlling information is controlling lines of communication, particularly access to key people. The person who controls lines of communication is likely to be granted favors from people who want access to those lines.

- Keep informed. It is politically important to keep informed. Successful leaders develop an information conduit to help them keep abreast, or ahead, of developments within the firm.

- Be courteous, pleasant, and positive. This not only helps your acquire power, it helps you retain power.

- Bring in an outside expert. To help justify their decisions, leaders often hire a consultant to conduct a study or cast an opinion. A consultant often supports the leader's position. Since the consultant is an outsider, the opinion will be perceived as objective.

- When given an assignment, try to achieve quick positive results. A display of dramatic results can help gain acceptance for one's efforts or those of the group.

- Ask satisfied customers to contact your boss. A favorable comment by a customer receives considerable weight because customer satisfaction is a top corporate priority.

- Ask advice. Asking advice on work-related topics builds relationships with other employees and is therefore an excellent leadership practice.

- Avoid political blunders. Committing these politically insensitive acts can also prevent one from attaining power. Leading blunders include strong criticism of a superior in a public forum and going around your boss with a complaint.

Use Sensitivity   You are using several of the political tactics discussed here and you are not achieving quick results. Perhaps you are not using enough sensitivity in implementing the political tactics. For example, you might be asking advice but in a way that suggests you have no intent of giving credit to others for the ideas. Try again, and explain that management will be made aware of all contributors to your report.

In this lesson you learned how to acquire power for yourself and your organizational unit, including the sources of power and political tactics to acquire power.

How to Lead by Example

In this lesson you will learn one of the most important techniques of an effective leader—leading by example.

The Meaning of Leading by Example

A simple but effective way of impressing and influencing group members is to lead by example. You act as a positive model so others can learn from your actions and attitudes.

Leading by Example Leading by example is influencing others by acting as a positive role model.

The ideal approach to leading by example is to be a "do as I say and do" leader. To be such a leader, do the following:

- Be consistent between your actions and words.

- Your actions and words should confirm, support, and clarify each other. Without such consistency, you lose credibility and people will stop respecting you as a leader.

- Develop a reputation for being the type of person you tell others to be.

SPECIFIC AREAS FOR LEADING BY EXAMPLE

Leading by example, or acting as a positive role model, is an effective leadership technique in many areas of managing. The following ten areas are particularly noteworthy.

COMMUNICATING ASPECTS OF THE ORGANIZATIONAL CULTURE

As a leader you can communicate values and expectations by your actions. Particularly well-suited to managing by example are actions showing loyalty, self-sacrifice, and service beyond the call of duty.

ADHERENCE TO POLICY

Most organizations have policies covering many aspects of employee behavior, such as absenteeism, tardiness, and honesty. Communicating these policies clearly and abiding by them is effective leadership.

GENERAL WORK HABITS

Group members will often look to you to set the work pace in terms of intensity, hours worked, and number of rest breaks. If you, as the leader, treat time as a precious resource, the workers in your area will likely pick up the pace of their work. Hours of work also have an impact. A leader who appears to be out of the office too frequently for nonwork reasons may soon find that staffers will be shortening their work week.

Demonstrating the Importance of Executing Unpleasant Tasks

Leading by example is an excellent vehicle for demonstrating that certain undesirable, or dangerous, tasks are of utmost importance. A manager from Xerox Corporation drove a snowmobile through a blizzard just to make sure that paychecks could be delivered on time.

Demonstrating Expert Power

To retain credibility as a leader it is necessary to demonstrate expert power from time to time. To demonstrate your expert power, you might occasionally take on a highly analytical or complex project.

Communicating the Meaning of Professional Behavior

What constitutes "professional behavior" varies widely from company to company. If you want to teach others the meaning of professional behavior, you have to first define it for yourself. Next, strive to act professionally. If you expect group members to act professionally around customers and visitors, you should act professionally around the same groups. Equally important, you should act professionally around staffers.

Create a good impression by expressing positive attitudes about the company, your job, customers, and the company's goods and services. If you are pessimistic, your negative attitudes will soon be reflected by members of the work group.

Physical Health, Safety, and Appearance

Organizations are quite health conscious, so it is important for you to talk about physical fitness and to appear fit yourself. It is also important to talk about and demonstrate safety.

Clothing and Grooming

The clothing you wear to work and how you are dressed often influences others. An accolade often given to well-respected managers and leaders is that they dress professionally.

Interpersonal Communication

You should set the style and tone of interpersonal communication. It impresses others if you can be forceful without screaming frequently and embarrassing or belittling others.

> **!** **Explaining Your Behavior**   You are leading by example when maintaining a positive outlook about the company and top management. Yet you still find too much griping and sniping among group members. Reinforce your leading by example with comments about why you behave the way you do. You might say, "I could moan and groan with the best of you. But instead, I try to appreciate the strengths of our employer. It's good for morale and productivity to be positive."

In this lesson you learned how to lead by example, including ten specific areas well-suited for the technique.

11

HOW TO USE INSPIRATIONAL APPEALS AND EMOTIONAL DISPLAYS

In this lesson you will learn how to use inspiration, an essential technique for becoming an effective leader. You also will learn how to make tactical use of displaying emotion.

HOW TO MAKE INSPIRATIONAL APPEALS

To be a leader, one has to inspire others to accomplish worthwhile goals. A natural method of inspiring others is to appeal to their emotions.

Here are a variety of techniques and ideas a leader can use to inspire others in the workplace.

Inspirational Appeal   An inspirational appeal is influencing another person to act in a particular way by triggering a strong emotional response in him or her.

IDENTIFY WHAT YOU WANT PEOPLE TO DO OR FEEL

The starting point in making an inspirational appeal is to identify what you want people to do or feel. Then you choose words, phrases, and ideas that fit your goal. As a manager you might be discouraged with the lax attitude people have toward their workplace's cleanliness and tidiness. Your goal is for the workers to maintain a near-spotless work area. So your inspirational appeal to fit the situation might include comments such as:

- "How would you people like to start looking like winners?"

- "A neighbor of mine visited our Japanese competitor last week. He couldn't help noticing that the factory looked as clean as a dealer showroom."

- "If we want others to think we are professionals, we have to start looking like professionals."

MAKE AN APPEAL TO STRONG VALUES

A basic tactic for inspiring others is to trigger thoughts related to strong values. Appealing to strong values is important because it leads to commitment to the task by group members. These strong values in the workplace include being the best, outperforming the competition, loyalty to the company, enhancing one's status, and being a good corporate citizen.

FORMULATE AN INSPIRING VISION

The vision a leader formulates should contribute to inspiring others. For example, the vision that inspires the employees at a Pepsi-Cola bottling plan in Springfield, Missouri emphasizes their wish to be one of the highest-quality Pepsi bottling plants in the world. But your vision should not sound the same as every other company's vision. Each company should come up with a unique vision.

Use High-Impact Words and Phrases

Each time you attempt an inspirational appeal, sprinkle your talk with high-impact words and phrases. Consult a thesaurus to enlarge your repertoire of high-impact words. Here is an example of using high-impact words: You want workers in your unit to become more safety conscious. In addition to stating that safety regulations must be observed, you might mention:

- "I don't want to hear about another crushed body in our factory."

- "Each month a few more computer users are crippling their wrists for life—all because of negligence on our part."

- "We need a safe, secure, and people-friendly environment."

Ask the Right Questions

An effective inspirational technique is to ask people questions that result in emotion-provoking answers. Your question prompts group members to give answers that stir their emotions and lead them to action. The question asked earlier in this lesson, "How would you people like to start looking like winners?" is a good example. Asking a question is often better than simply making a statement such as, "I would like you people to start acting like winners." The reason is that answering a question results in more mental activity and commitment than simply listening to a message.

INSPIRE PEOPLE WITH SUCCESS STORIES

Success stories are a natural way of inspiring others to extend themselves. Browse through media sources and books for stories about ordinary people who rose to great heights of achievement. People are often inspired by stories of people similar to them who began a business in their kitchen or garage and built it into a national or world leader. For example, Ragu, a leading pasta sauce, had its humble origins in someone's kitchen.

APPEAL TO MULTIPLE SENSES

Another tactic for making an inspirational appeal is to appeal to more than one sense. You want people to hear your message, but you also want them to see it, feel it, touch it, and taste it. As in the use of visual imagery, encourage people to imagine the total experience of achieving the goal you believe is important. The manager facing an extraordinarily difficult deadline might inspire the group to achieve the goal with such statements as:

- "Can you imagine what it will *look* like to see 150,000 of these units packaged and loaded into trucks?"

- "Just think of how your family members will *squeal* with delight when you tell them you have earned a bonus."

- "Imagine how *relaxed* your body will feel after we have achieved this momentous accomplishment?"

- "We are on the way to our most profitable year in a decade. Join me in *tasting* victory."

 Include a Concrete Plan of Action   To achieve rapid results with your inspirational appeals, follow up stirred emotions with a concrete plan of action.

How to Make Tactical Use of Emotional Displays

Part of inspiring people is to make tactical use of emotional displays. By showing your emotions and feelings for effect, you are using them in a tactical, planned manner.

The emotions a leader displays for effect can be negative or positive. Table-thumping works because it shows people you are serious, and triggers an emotional response in them. Outbursts of positive emotion are also helpful in triggering an emotional response from workers. Cheering wildly, an outburst of laughter, or crying with joy can all give a boost to leadership effectiveness.

The following suggestions will help you make good use of displays of emotion and feeling:

- Save emotional displays for rare occasions. Otherwise you will appear to be emotionally volatile, and perhaps unfit for your leadership role.

- Be explicit about your feelings. Make statements such as, "I'm so disappointed that we missed our target again" or "I feel incredibly good that we produced 30 percent beyond what anybody imagined we could."

- Concentrate so that your nervous system matches your emotion. For example, if your eyes widen and blood rushes to your skin when you are screaming, you will be more effective than if you don't feel angry inside.

- Practice showing positive and negative emotion even when you don't feel that way inside. An inspirational leader can flip the toggle switch for emotional displays as needed.

In this lesson you learned some techniques to inspire others by appealing to their emotions and feelings, including how to best use emotional displays.

12

How to Manipulate Others Ethically

In this lesson you will learn how to influence others in a subtle, indirect way, often referred to as manipulation.

Why Manipulation Is Important for Leadership

Many people cringe when they hear or read the term "manipulation," especially in relation to leadership. If leaders are to supposed to be models of ethics and trustworthiness, how can they be manipulative at the same time? The answer depends on how you define manipulation.

Suppose you perceive manipulation to be a devious influence tactic in which you trick the unsuspecting target into doing something he or she never wanted to do. Furthermore, what you get the person to do is against that individual's best interests. There is no question that an effective leader should not engage in that type of manipulation.

Suppose instead that you perceive manipulation to be a subtle influence tactic that may be necessary to help people achieve ends that will benefit both them and the organization.

Manipulation is sometimes used because more direct influence tactics may not be effective in a given circumstance. Manipulation therefore has an important place in leadership given that a leader's major job is to influence others.

Used unethically, however, you can be sure that such tactics will backfire, undermining the leader's credibility and ability to influence others.

 Manipulation   Manipulation, as described here, is an indirect, subtle, and covert method of influencing others that may or may not involve some deception.

TECHNIQUES OF MANIPULATION TO CONSIDER

A challenge in applying manipulation is that specific techniques are rarely spelled out. People often say, "I'm being manipulated," but they fail to describe exactly what is happening to them. What follows are some manipulation techniques that leaders will find useful.

THE BANDWAGON TECHNIQUE

Everyone who has been exposed to advertising has experienced the bandwagon technique. This technique influences another person by pointing out that others are engaging in the activity you are prescribing. Here's an example of the bandwagon technique:

Sherri is the manager of information systems. Part of her job is to lead the organization toward better use of information technology. Sherri's boss is dragging his heels on investing money in a World Wide Web page. To overcome her boss's resistance, Sherri informs her boss, "I've done some research on the World Wide Web. We're the only company our size lacking a Web site. What should we do next?" Her boss replies, "If that's the case, let's set one up right away." To make effective use of the bandwagon technique, consider the following:

- Point to a specific reference group (such as other companies similar in size to yours), rather than the vague "everybody is doing it."

- Avoid using the technique with people who pride themselves in being nonconformists. These people prefer to resist doing what everybody else is doing.

- Be specific about what you want your influence target to do. Tell him or her what you expect but not necessarily how to do it.

- Make your influence target feel good about having moved in the desired direction. State that he or she has made a wise decision.

Joking and Kidding

Good-natured kidding is especially effective when a straightforward statement might be interpreted as harsh criticism. Joking or kidding can thus get the message across and lower the risk that the person the leader is trying to influence will be angry with the leader doing the influencing.

Here is an example of joking and kidding to influence a procrastinating team member to become more prompt:

> *Team Leader:* It looks like I made a little error when I gave you the date for the completion of your input to the project.

Team Member: I didn't know you made an error. You told me June 30.

Team Leader: Yes, but since it's now July 15, I assume I must have told you June 30 of next year.

Team Member: (Laughs) I feel terrible. Give me two more days, and my portion will be done.

The leader was criticizing the team member in such a gentle way that this person got the point without becoming defensive.

Manipulation Can Strengthen Your Influence
Joking and kidding is particularly useful when you are trying to influence somebody over whom you have little or no formal authority. If you need to get a higher authority to back you up to get somebody to act, you will appear weak. So an indirect (or manipulative) influence tactic may be useful.

IMPLIED BENEFIT

Using the implied-benefit technique, the influencer alludes to certain advantages that may be forthcoming from complying with his or her demands. For example, some workers might be resisting a six-month assignment to a task force that they believe will be boring and unproductive. The influencer states, "This task force *could* be a great opportunity. Performing well on a task force is a wonderful way to get noticed by higher management."

The reluctant group members now accept the task force assignment. If any one of them benefits professionally, the leader will have manipulated this individual into an activity that helps the organization but is also personally rewarding.

DEBASEMENT

To use debasement, a person demeans or insults himself to control the behavior of the other person. It's a way of insulting yourself so the other person feels sorry for you. Out of guilt or strong compassion, the person you are trying to influence grants a concession or complies with your demands. Here is an example of debasement: A higher-ranking executive wants an operations manager to trim down a capital budget request for next year. The executive says, "I know I'm not an expert in operations, and that you know ten times as much as I do about the manufacturing process, but I do know we don't have enough money in the budget to do everything. Could you find any way of cutting back your request that would not hurt productivity?"

BUILDING A CLOSE RELATIONSHIP

Leadership involves building warm relationships with people, but sometimes these relationships are manipulative. In its simplest form, a manager builds a personal relationship with a higher-ranking manager or a group member. The relationships involve outside-of-work social events, including members becoming friends. The manager can now exert the following types of indirect influence:

- It will be more difficult for the higher-ranking manager to turn down a budget request since it came from a personal friend.

- The manager is at an advantage in staying off the hit list during the next downsizing.

- The group member will be more willing to go along with requests for performing beyond the call of duty.

CO-OPTATION (GETTING THE ENEMY TO JOIN YOU)

A common form of manipulation at higher levels in organizations is called co-optation. This involves converting an individual or group to your way of thinking by having the people join forces with you, even temporarily.

Assume that a marketing manager was concerned that the finance department might oppose funding for his new program, to be launched next year. The marketing manager would then invite an influential member of the finance department to serve on a cross-functional team working on the new program. The expectation is that as a result of working on the program, the finance person would become an ally. An ally would then not shoot down a proposal from her friends in marketing. Co-optation has these advantages:

- It's an easy and inexpensive way to get an individual's or group's support.

- It fits the spirit of the times of working with people from outside your own department.

- It involves no bribes or false promises.

SHAM PARTICIPATION (MAKE THEM THINK IT'S THEIR IDEA)

We've saved the form of manipulation most widely practiced by leaders for last. The leader has a useful idea she wants the group to implement. Yet in the culture of participative management and team management, the leader knows that group members expect to participate in decision making. The leader then conducts a series of meetings to "bat around ideas for a new system."

During the meetings, the manager gets excited about suggestions that fit her system. She often submits an idea that leads
people to think in the direction she wants, such as specifying
criteria that point to her system. After collecting input from
group members, she presents a new system that "reflects the
collective thinking of the group." The new system works well,
and group members are satisfied that they contributed so
heavily to its development. It has been said that a leader has
done an outstanding job when group members say, "We did it
ourselves."

> **!** **Admit to Constructive Manipulation**   After using
> an indirect influence tactic, a group member says
> in an angry tone, "Are you manipulating me?" An
> effective answer might be, "You're right. As a
> leader, I'm trying to help you achieve a goal that
> will help you and the company. If you call that ma-
> nipulation, I am manipulating you."

In this lesson you learned how to influence others in a subtle,
indirect way, often referred to as manipulation.

GAINING THE SUPPORT OF GROUP MEMBERS

In this lesson you will learn methods you can use to gain the support of group members so you can enhance your leadership effectiveness.

PROJECT CONFIDENCE IN GROUP MEMBERS

A subtle way to impress group members is to show through your actions and spontaneous comments that you believe in them. Assume that a team member says to you, "I'll get those figures for you by Friday." If you say "That's good" with a skeptical expression, the team member will not think you have much confidence in him or her. If you accompany your comment "That's good" with a convincing facial expression, then you can expect the team member will be impressed that you believe in him or her.

Projecting confidence in team members impresses them so much that they are likely to live up to your expectations. Sometimes this is known as a self-fulfilling prophecy. When you look and speak as if you expect team members to succeed, you can capitalize on the potency of the self-fulfilling prophecy.

Self-Fulfilling Prophecy   A self-fulfilling prophecy is a way of saying that when people believe
something to be true, they act in ways to make it
come true for them.

DELEGATE SOME EXCITING ASSIGNMENTS

Most managers can readily hand over burdensome, unexcit-
ing, unglamorous, or hazardous assignments to a group member. An impressive delegator is a manager who turns over an
exciting, glamorous, and safe assignment to somebody on the
team.

Delegating exciting assignments builds loyalty among group
members. People usually remember who made their work
life better and respond by forming an emotional tie with that
person.

GIVE AND SOLICIT FEEDBACK

Many employees complain that they work in a no-feedback
environment. You can therefore impress group members by
giving them feedback on the work they perform for you. Positive feedback builds a good relationship. Soliciting feedback is
also an effective leadership technique. Suggestions for giving
and receiving feedback include:

- Provide specific feedback. Instead of making gener-
  alizations about an improvement area for another
  person, pinpoint areas of concern.

- Strive to give negative feedback on actions and be-haviors rather than personality traits. For example, it is better to state that a group member made five mis-takes in a report than to tell the person "you're sloppy."

- Look at feedback from group members as a gift, and dig for more details after hearing the initial feedback. "I appreciate your honesty in making those com-ments. What would you suggest I do to improve?"

- Even if you are not in the mood, strive to give feed-back as needed. Positive feedback is a great motivator and negative feedback is an important vehicle for changing behavior.

RESPECT SENIORITY

Despite tough laws against age discrimination, many employ-ees and job candidates age 50 and older believe that their age is a liability. In such a climate, showing appreciation for se-niority will help you gain the support of group members. Showing respect for seniority in this context means that you appreciate the employee's long-term contribution. Appreciat-ing seniority increases in importance when you are a young, newly appointed manager. Ways to show respect for seniority include:

- When asking a senior person a question, sometimes begin with the phrase, "Based on your experience...."

- Avoid stereotypes about veteran workers such as as-suming they are not interested in learning new technology or that they are not well equipped for imaginative thinking.

PROMOTE YOUR GROUP THROUGHOUT THE ORGANIZATION

You will strengthen your relationship with team members if you are an ardent spokesperson for the group throughout the organization. Collect glory for the group as well as for yourself and you will develop loyal supporters. When speaking to managers or group members from other departments, point factually to your group's achievements. Of paramount importance, let upper management know how much your group is in tune with organizational goals.

BE HUMANISTIC

A major concern in an era of downsizing, mergers, and acquisitions is that employers have little regard for the welfare of individual workers. You can capitalize on employee concerns about corporate insensitivity by being purposely humanistic. Show an interest in the nonwork aspects of the lives of group members without neglecting concern about good performance.

 Humanistic   A humanistic manager shows a strong concern for human interests, value, and dignity.

Being humanistic can include many actions and attitudes that respond to the emotions and feelings of group members. Here is a list of some humanistic management and leadership practices:

- Ask group members how company and job expectations mesh with their personal values.

- Initiate a dress-down day that encourages employees to dress in the type of clothing they would ordinarily wear doing household chores or exercise.

- Ask group members what you might be able to do to make their job easier.

- Conduct a group meeting to discuss all the programs the company offers that could possibly make life easier for employees.

- Conduct a luncheon discussion about the major sources of work stress and what can be done about them.

- Write a personal note at midyear to high-contributing workers expressing appreciation for their help in keeping the company in business.

- Give group members proper credit for their ideas that you use. A major employee complaint is that managers use their ideas without giving appropriate credit.

- Invest a couple of hours per month listening to the personal problems and complaints of employees. Let them ventilate about their confusion and anger, but avoid becoming their counselor.

- Pay a compliment at least once a month to group members. An easy, natural one is "Thanks for the nice job you did for me the other day."

SOLICIT OPINIONS BEFORE TAKING ACTIONS

Participative management has become ingrained into the culture of organizations. Whether you merely consult with group members or get their full approval before taking action, the result is similar—people will be pleased that they were included in the decision-making process. The result will usually be better support for you and an interest in helping you implement the decision.

LET BAD IDEAS DOWN GENTLY

One of the problems with encouraging people to participate in decision making is that you often wind up with some unusable suggestions. If you flatly reject all the suggestions you receive from group members, they perceive you as not really interested in what they have to say. If you are tactful about turning down the worst ideas, you will at least create the impression of being a good listener. Here are two examples of diplomatically rejecting ideas from group members:

- "You say that we could save considerable money by eliminating executive bonuses. The best I can do for now is to bring that idea to the next management meeting."

- "You recommend that the company could reduce medical insurance costs in the long run by making first-aid training mandatory for every employee. I'll number and date your idea, and keep it on file for review at our next budget meeting."

In this lesson you learned several methods for gaining the support of group members.

14

How to Build Teamwork

In this lesson you will learn how to be successful at one of a leader's most important challenges—building teamwork.

Encourage Team Members to Treat Each Other as if They Were External Customers

A high-powered strategy for building teamwork is to encourage team members to treat each other as if they were external (paying) customers. Treating each other as customers fosters cooperative behavior and politeness. Treating team members as customers would involve group members taking such actions as:

- Inviting a team member to lunch just to maintain a working relationship.

- Asking a teammate if you could help her solve a difficult problem.

- Asking a teammate exactly the kind of input he needed so you could do an outstanding job of helping him.

Get People to Trust Each Other

Mutual trust is a bedrock condition for high levels of team-work and cooperation. If team members don't trust each other, they will hold back on full mutual cooperation. Trust takes time to develop, but here are several tactics you can use to build trust:

- Encourage team members to give honest feedback to each other, such as saying, "You correct me so often when I'm talking that I feel uneasy working with you."

- Hold candid meetings. Candor leads to trust because openly expressing one's opinions leads others to think the person tends not to hide opinions and information.

- Encourage team members to talk about the other things they do on the job outside of shared team activities.

Encourage Team Members to Share Ideas

Idea sharing is a heavy-duty tactic for developing teamwork because the exchange of information requires a high level of cooperation.

A straightforward approach to idea sharing is to reserve a portion of each group meeting for idea sharing or information exchange. During this portion of the meeting the members might also be encouraged to provide constructive feedback to each other.

ALLOW FOR PHYSICAL PROXIMITY AMONG MEMBERS

You can enhance group cohesiveness, and therefore teamwork, when team members are located close together and can interact frequently and easily. Frequent interaction often leads to camaraderie and a feeling of belongingness. Physical proximity can be achieved through means such as:

- Establishing a shared physical facility such as a conference room, research library, or beverage lounge.

- Using the modern type of modular furniture whereby individual cubicles can be temporarily converted into a common work area.

- Using office landscaping rather than offices with doors (as is becoming almost standard practice except for executives).

GET THE TEAM TO SPEND TIME TOGETHER

A team becomes more cohesive as its members spend more time together. Team meetings are obviously important, particularly when they involve joint problem solving. Group breakfasts, luncheons, and after-hours parties are also opportunities for spending time together. As a manager, however, you have to be careful not to extend the already demanding work week for professionals.

Make Frequent Use of Terms and Phrases that Support Teamwork

A team is designed to be a democratic structure in which rank and other status differences are not so pronounced. Emphasizing the words *team members* or *teammates*, and de-emphasizing the words *subordinates, employees,* and *direct reports* helps promote the idea of teamwork. Referring to yourself as the *team leader, coach,* or *facilitator* is also better than the title *department manager*.

Make frequent use of the terms *we* and *us*, especially when referring to problems and accomplishments. You enhance teamwork when team members think of the manager as working with them in solving problems.

Emphasize the Fact that Yours Is a Winning Team

Whether winning teams create good teamwork or the reverse, it pays to emphasize that yours is a winning team. Remind team members frequently of what your team is doing that is above average and consequently why they belong to a winning team.

Reward Contributions to Team Goals

For the group to develop a strong team spirit, individuals must feel a sense of mutual accountability. Team members should be given frequent reminders of what they are doing right and encouraged for actions that contribute to team goals.

EMPHASIZE GROUP RECOGNITION

Giving rewards for group accomplishment reinforces teamwork because people receive rewards for what they have
achieved collaboratively. The recognition accompanying the
reward should emphasize the team's value to the organization,
rather than to the individual. Three examples of team recognition follow:

- A display wall or electronic bulletin board for
  postings related to team activities, such as certificates
  of accomplishment, schedules, and miscellaneous
  announcements.

- Team logos on items, such as identifying T-shirts,
  athletic caps, mugs, jackets, key rings, sport bags,
  and business cards.

- Celebrations to mark milestones, such as first-time
  activities, quality improvements, productivity improvements, cost savings, and high levels of customer satisfaction.

- An end-of-year memo to the team, and to top management, summarizing the team's accomplishments
  for the year.

CREATE OPPORTUNITIES FOR OTHERS

If the team leader hogs the best opportunities, assignments,
and credits, it will dampen team spirit and team performance.
One of a leader's biggest challenges is to provide opportunities
for the team leader and team members to perform well. The
challenge is more acute when the leader is a person with a
strong track record, and the other team members are at an
earlier career stage. Consider these ideas for creating opportunities for others:

- If you have an opportunity to visit a top executive or a key customer, bring along a team member. Assign him or her a meaningful role such as presenting technical details.

- Grant the authority to the group to work on a major problem with a minimum of your input and direction.

- Welcome all input from team members to encourage even modest contributions.

ENGAGE IN TASKS PERFORMED BY THE TEAM

An effective team leader performs many of the tasks performed by team members, including analytical work, calling on accounts, and crunching numbers. The idealized version of a leader who spends all of his or her time formulating visions, crafting strategic plans, and inspiring others through charisma does not fit team leadership.

The team leader does engage in some work that is strictly the leader's responsibility, such as arriving at a final decision after listening to group input. Yet much of the team leader's job overlaps with that of team members, at least in groups where team spirit or productivity are high.

INTRODUCE HUMOR WITH APPROPRIATE FREQUENCY

Humor and laughter are excellent vehicles for building team spirit when used with appropriate frequency. Shared laughter helps build camaraderie. The group needs to laugh together to raise morale, to increase the fun associated with the team task, and to stimulate creativity.

ENCOURAGE THE USE OF IN-GROUP JARGON

Conventional wisdom is that jargon should be minimized in business. Yet liberal use of jargon among team members enhances team spirit because it sets the team apart from others in the organization. When dealing with outsiders, team members can then follow the principle of minimizing jargon.

The more specialized the work of the team, the greater the effectiveness of jargon. For example, a team performing legal work might refer to a knowledgeable judge as a "jurist." (Many outsiders would think a jurist is a member of the jury!)

USE TEAM INCENTIVES

A key strategy for encouraging teamwork is to reward the team as well as individual members. The most convincing team incentive is to calculate compensation partially on the basis of team results. Team incentives build teamwork because the team must perform well for individuals to receive their share of the merit pay given to the team.

 Helping the Isolated Team Member You have tried hard to promote teamwork within your group, yet one of the members stays isolated from the group. Speak to that person about the problem. Listen to his or her explanation about not working more closely with the group. Ask what you can do to help.

In this lesson you learned some strategies and tactics for fostering teamwork within your group.

How to Be a Nurturing Leader

In this lesson you will learn how to be the type of leader who nurtures group members, thereby contributing to their growth and development.

What It Means to Be a Nurturing Leader

You nurture along team members, helping them to grow and develop. The group members who want to be nurtured will become your strong supporters. It will be easy for you to spot the people who don't want to be nurtured. They will back away mentally when you attempt to help them or try to get too close to them emotionally.

Nurturing is a fuzzy word, but it can be translated into specific practices such as:

- Having a genuine concern for the welfare of group members is the starting point.

- Investing substantial time into listening to the work problems of group members.

- Investing an adequate amount of time in listening to the personal problems of group members.

- Demonstrate by your comments that you worry about the setbacks and disappointments of group members.

- Congratulate group members regularly when they demonstrate skill development.

- Use your power to help group members resolve bothersome problems.

 Nurturing Leader   A nurturing leader is one who actively promotes the growth of group members in terms of skills, knowledge, and emotional cohesion.

RECOGNIZE THAT MOST PEOPLE HAVE GROWTH NEEDS

To be a nurturing leader you have to recognize that almost everybody has a need for self-fulfillment, although people vary in the extent of this need. You might engage in interactions with group members such as sharing new skills with them, clipping relevant news articles, or telling them about an important new Internet file you've discovered.

PLAY THE MENTOR ROLE

Serving as a mentor is an excellent way to foster the development of group members. As a mentor, you nurture your protege. To be a mentor, you can engage in a wide range of helping behaviors, all related to being a trusted friend, coach, and teacher. A mentor typically helps along a person of lower rank, but the new trend is to be a mentor to a peer. To prepare you for mentoring a group member (or a peer), a list of specific mentoring actions follows:

- As a sponsor, a mentor actively nominates somebody else for promotions, worthwhile transfers, and interesting temporary assignments.

- As a coach, a mentor gives on-the-spot advice to the protege to help him or her improve skills.

- A mentor might shield a junior person from potentially harmful situations or from a difficult higher-level manager.

- A mentor will look for the opportunity to give the protege challenging assignments and then provide feedback on performance.

- The mentor sometimes refers the protege to resources inside and outside the company to help with a particular problem.

- A mentor can be helpful just by giving support and encouragement. In turn, the protege is supposed to support the mentor by offering compliments and defending the mentor's ideas.

- A mentor listens to the protege's problems and offers advice, thus engaging in some light counseling.

- A mentor is, above all, a trusted friend, and the friendship extends two ways.

- Mentors help their proteges solve problems by themselves and make their own discoveries.

- A general-purpose function of the mentor is to help the protege learn the ropes. This translates into explaining the values and dos and don'ts of the organization.

Mentoring on the Run   Mentoring can be a time-consuming process involving lengthy discussions, lunches, and dinners with a protege. Yet effective mentoring can also take place with one-minute in-person suggestions, e-mail messages, and brief phone calls. After attending a meeting with your protege, you might give that person a quick comment on how well he or she performed in the meeting—along with a suggestion for improvement.

BE A ROLE MODEL FOR OTHERS

Your skill in leading by example can indirectly help you be a nurturing leader. By serving as a role model, you can help another person develop. The person deliberately, or without realizing it directly, picks up positive ideas from you on how to function well in a work environment. Some things that make you a role model include:

- A strong work ethic
- Job expertise
- Personal warmth
- Good speaking ability
- Outstanding facility with information technology
- Strong business ethics

ENGAGE IN SUPPORTIVE COMMUNICATION

Communicating powerfully and dramatically facilitates influencing and inspiring people. A more mellow type of communication is needed to help people develop and grow. A leader who uses supportive communication nurtures group members and brings out their best.

Supportive Communication Supportive communication is a communication style that delivers the message accurately and supports or enhances the relationship between two parties.

Supportive communication has seven principles or characteristics:

1. Supportive communication is problem-oriented, not person-oriented. Most people are more receptive to a discussion of what can be done to change a work method than to change them.

2. Supportive communication is based on verbal and nonverbal communication being congruent. This means your words, body language, and facial expressions are all consistent with one another and that you don't send any mixed messages.

Mixed Message A mixed message comes about when you say one thing but your tone and body language say something else. For example, if you say "I really trust you," but you have your arms folded and a scowl on your face, that's definitely a mixed message.

3. Supportive communication validates rather than invalidates people. Validating communication makes a person feel good because it accepts the presence, uniqueness, and importance of the other person.

4. Supportive communication is specific, not general. As described in Lesson 13, most people benefit more from specific rather than general feedback.

5. Supportive communication is linked logically to previous messages, thus enhancing communication. When communication has a logical link to what has just been said it is easier for group members to follow the leader's thoughts.

6. Supportive communication is owned, not disowned. Effective communicators take responsibility for what they say and don't attribute the authority behind their ideas to another person. The effective leader might say, "I want everybody to work ten extra hours per week during this crunch period." The less-effective leader might say, "The company wants everybody to work ten extra hours per week during this crunch period."

7. Supportive communication requires listening as well as sending messages. The relationship between two parties can't be enhanced unless both listen to each other. In addition, a key strategy for helping people grow and develop is to allow them to be heard.

Know When to Back Off A nurturing leader makes many contributions to people, organizations, and society. Yet some independent-minded people may resist being nurtured. In these cases, the best approach is to be a good role model for that person. Save your energy for nurturing others who want your help.

In this lesson you learned a variety of approaches to being the type of leader who fosters the growth and development of group members.

16

How to Be a
Good Coach

*In this lesson you will learn how to enhance your effectiveness in a
basic aspect of leadership—coaching group members to higher levels
of performance.*

 Coaching Coaching helps group members perform better; it can take place on the spot or in a
formal discussion, and usually includes making
suggestions.

Observe the Discrepancies
Between Desired and Actual
Performance

A substantial part of your impact as a leader stems from your
ability to coach group members. In the traditional view,
coaching deals with performance problems such as low productivity, absenteeism and tardiness, and poor safety practices.
Yet coaching also includes helping satisfactory and high-level
performers reach new heights of achievement.

Whether you are coaching to fix a serious problem or to boost performance, coaching begins with observing the discrepancies between desired and actual performance.

USE A GOOD OPENING STATEMENT

Your coaching activity can consist of a formal, sit-down session or an impromptu meeting in the group member's work area.

Get to the heart of the issue quickly but tactfully, without disguising the purpose of the discussion. Beginning the session with a compliment may not be effective. The problem is that the person being coached develops the mental set that no problem of consequence exists. Here are some effective opening statements to use as a guide:

- "I've asked you to meet with me because I'm concerned about how often your reports are late. I hope we can work this problem out together."

- "I'm concerned about your sales being flat for so many months. I want us to figure out together how you can get off this plateau. You're doing fine, but I know you can do great."

ESTABLISH REALISTIC IMPROVEMENT GOALS

The fact that you are coaching somebody else means that in your opinion the person needs to achieve a higher level of performance. If improvement goals are too high, such as tripling productivity in 30 days, the group member is likely to fail and become frustrated. If improvement goals are too low, the group member's performance may not improve fast enough. A realistic improvement goal pushes a person, but does not set him or her up for failure.

You, as the leader, may help the group member set realistic improvement goals by encouraging discussion of each one. Setting realistic goals does not mean you are giving up on performance standards that are important to the company. It just means that the worker cannot reach the performance level you want in one jump.

EXPLAIN VALID REASONS FOR SOLVING THE PROBLEM

Your stature as a leader will sometimes be sufficient to convince the person you're coaching that improvement is necessary. In many situations, however, justifying your request with a solid business reason will be more convincing. Not all workers are aware of the organizational consequences of their below-standard performance. Several examples of valid business reasons to justify the need for performance improvement are:

- "Our costs per sale have jumped 25 percent in the last year. This is why we need higher productivity from each sales person."

- "If most employees were consistently tardy, the productivity drain on the company would be enormous. If every employee lost three hours of productivity per year because of tardiness, the company would have a productivity drain of 150,000 hours of work per year."

- "If you could develop just one more breakthrough idea per year, our product-design group would be world-class."

ENGAGE IN ACTIVE LISTENING

Active listening is an essential ingredient in any coaching session. An active listener tries to grasp both the facts of what is said and the feelings behind the words. Observing the group member's nonverbal communication is another part of active listening. The leader must also be patient and not poised for a rebuttal to any differences of opinion between him or her and the group member.

Active Listening   Active listening is listening for full meaning, without making premature judgments or interpretations.

Practicing a few basic techniques will help you become an active listener:

- Part of being a good listener is encouraging the person being coached to talk about his or her performance. Asking open-ended questions facilitates a flow of conversation.

Open-ended Question   An open-ended question is one that requires explanation rather than just a yes or no answer.

- A good coach is adept at reflecting feelings. The leader's reflection of feelings communicates the fact that he or she understands the problem. Feeling understood, the group member might be better motivated to improve.

- A good coach also reflects content or meaning. An effective way of reflecting meaning is to rephrase and summarize concisely what the group member is saying. A poorly performing group member might say: "The reason that I've fallen so far behind is that our company has turned into a bureaucratic nightmare. I have forms to fill out all day long." You might respond: "You're falling so far behind because you have so many forms that require attention." The group member might then respond: "That's exactly what I mean. I'm glad you understand my problem."

- After you have listened to a person for a while, give your interpretation of what he or she has said. You can use this interpretation to give the person you're coaching insight into the nature of the problem.

GIVE SOME CONSTRUCTIVE ADVICE

Too much advice giving interferes with two-way communication, yet some advice can lead to improved performance. Recognize also that giving expert advice is an important leadership role. Assist the person you're coaching to answer the question, "What can I do about this problem?" Advice in the form of a question or suppositional statement is often effective.

GIVE EMOTIONAL SUPPORT

By being helpful and constructive, you provide much-needed emotional support to the person who needs help in improving job performance. A coaching session should not be an interrogation. An effective way of providing emotional support is to use positive rather than negative motivators. For example, as a team leader you might say to a team member, "Your job performance is above average right now. Yet if you learn how to analyze manufacturing costs, you will be eligible for an outstanding performance review."

A negative motivator, giving no emotional support, on the same topic might be, "If you don't learn how to analyze manufacturing costs, you're going to get zapped on your performance review."

HELP OVERCOME BARRIERS TO GOOD PERFORMANCE

Many of the problems of poor work performance are caused by factors beyond a worker's control. By showing a willingness to intervene in such problems, the leader displays a helpful and constructive attitude and gives emotional support. A sampling of the type of factors beyond a worker's control that could benefit from intervention by the manager includes:

- Insufficient support staff to handle a peak workload.

- Not having enough equipment for the work that needs to be done, which leads to employees waiting to use equipment, and lowered productivity.

- The presence of a hostile, uncooperative co-worker who drags down group productivity.

- Lack of cooperation by members of another department.

ALLOW FOR MODELING OF DESIRED PERFORMANCE AND BEHAVIOR

An effective coaching technique is to show the person being coached an example of what constitutes the desired behavior.

A customer service manager was harsh with customers when facing heavy pressure. One way the boss coached the service manager was for the boss to take over the manager's desk during a busy period. The service manager then watched the boss deal tactfully with demanding customers.

Gain a Commitment to Change

Gaining a commitment to change is yet another important part of coaching. Unless the leader receives a commitment from the group member to carry through with the proposed solution to a problem, the member may not improve performance.

An experienced manager/coach develops an intuitive feel for when workers are serious about improving their performance. One clue that commitment to change is lacking is if a group member is overly enthusiastic about the need for change. Another is agreeing to change without a display of emotion.

Suppose that as part of a process redesign, the team agrees to stop writing confirmation letters about orders. (The new procedure saves time by electronically transmitting confirmation of orders on standard forms stored in the computer.) Yet one of the inside sales representatives continues to slow down the process by mailing out confirmation letters. You coach the representative about the problem. At the end of the session he says, "OK, sure," with a disinterested expression. You will probably have to monitor his performance closely because he is likely not yet committed to the change.

Be More Explicit Next Time   You coached a group member about a problem or lost opportunity, yet his or her behavior has not changed. Hold another session or on-the-spot discussion with the person. Your message and suggestions may not have sunk in the first time because performance improvement is such an emotional topic.

In this lesson you learned many actions and techniques that will enable you to carry out effectively the coaching aspect of leadership.

17

How to Minimize Micromanagement

In this lesson you will learn how to minimize micromanagement, a problem facing many dynamic, results-oriented leaders.

Begin by Understanding the Nature of Micromanagement

In today's workplace it is an insult to call a leader a micromanager. A manager or leader who closely monitors the work of group members is thought to be out of touch with empowerment. Yet in reality, many successful leaders make suggestions about the technical details of the work they oversee. Many top automotive executives, for example, have strong opinions about automobile design.

 Micromanagement Micromanagement is the close monitoring of most aspects of group member activities by the manager or leader.

The true issue is finding the right balance between providing no leadership or supervision versus managing down to the smallest detail. As a tentative guideline, you know you are micromanaging when you regularly do such things as:

- Ask to review the To Do list of group members.

- Require that group members punch in and punch out for lunch.

- Review all petty cash expenses.

- Require daily progress reports from each member of the department.

- Study carefully the computer printout of telephone calls made by people in the department.

- Edit and proofread all reports sent outside the group.

- Visit each member of the group at his or her work area at least once per day.

- Accompany a group member when he or she visits a customer or client for the first time.

- Conduct three-hour performance appraisals.

- Dictate what software group members should use to prepare reports.

- Rarely, if ever, ask group members to contribute agenda items for a staff meeting.

- Investigate in person a site chosen for a department party before giving approval.

- Make food and exercise recommendations to group members.

- Give unsolicited advice to group members about managing their personal finances.

RECOGNIZE THAT A MANAGER IS A COACH, NOT A PLAYER

To avoid micromanagement, and to be an effective delegator at the same time, the manager must understand the difference between being a coach and a player. The leader can still perform some of the tasks, but the emphasis is on showing other people on how to accomplish work and then motivating them to sustain their performance. If a player (team member) makes a mistake the coach does not take over, but instead offers a constructive suggestion.

STEP BACK FROM THE DETAILS

A major hurdle in overcoming micromanagement is stepping back from the details and letting other people take care of them. If a leader can't let go of details, he or she will always be a micromanager. To help step back from details, keep these attitudes in mind:

- "I can't do everything, so it is only natural that team members are taking care of important details."

- "Even if I have more experience in doing (this particular task), if I take over most of the job, I would be performing more like an individual contributor than a leader."

- "I will satisfy my interest in doing technical work by taking on an occasional project by myself."

- "I can practice my expertise by acting as a consultant to a group member who asks for help, but I won't attempt to take over his or her role."

TRUST OTHERS

It is difficult to avoid micromanagement if the leader does not trust workers. Frequent checking is a form of micromanagement and interferes with delegation. Group members lose initiative and begin to guess what the leader would do in this particular situation. If this happens, creative problem-solving may be limited.

BE WILLING TO LET OTHERS MAKE MISTAKES

If people don't make occasional mistakes, it is because they are not taking risks. When a manager avoids micromanagement (and therefore delegates freely), people will make some mistakes as they learn their new assignments. Many successful executives regard these mistakes as investments in the education and training of group members.

GRANT PEOPLE SUFFICIENT AUTHORITY TO ACCOMPLISH THEIR TASKS

To accomplish tasks or assignments, the group member must have the authority to do certain things without constantly checking with the leader. To cite an example, if a manager is given the responsibility for a crash project, the manager should be able to hire temporary workers without checking with the boss.

Frequent checking with the manager breeds micromanagement because the manager feels obliged to review items before approving them. The more interaction a group member has with you, the greater the temptation for micromanaging.

Curb Your Tendencies Toward Perfectionism

Leaders who are perfectionists are uncomfortable with delegation because control over how the job is performed is taken out of their hands. As a result, the perfectionist is likely to micromanage. Perfectionists who do delegate tend to carefully monitor the work of group members assigned the work and pester them to conform. The pestering is often perceived as micromanagement.

Overcome the Attitude, "I Can Handle it Better Than You"

Managers often believe they can perform the delegated assignment better than the group member. As a result of this attitude, they don't project confidence in the worker's ability to perform the delegated task. The worker then feels that he or she is being watched too closely. As a consequence, the worker feels that he or she is being micromanaged.

Avoid Upward Delegation

Upward delegation occurs when a group member delegates his or her assigned work to the manager. A group member will often ask for advice from the manager, or how to solve a problem. If the manager accepts the work coming back to him or her, the manager has been trapped into micromanagement. Remember that micromanagement can be undesirable even if it is initiated by a group member.

Be a Macromanager   This entire lesson has been a timesaver tip. A leader who is a macromanager (the opposite of a micromanager) has much more time for performing high-level leadership work. For example, if you are busy checking expense accounts you have less time for planning and inspiring others.

Intervene in an Emergency   Your first attempts at avoiding micromanagement aren't working. You are gritting your teeth while a group member is driving a key project over a cliff. Intervene if you must, but then identify another delegated task that you will absolutely not micromanage. It takes time to break the micromanaging habit, and you should pick your spots at first.

In this lesson you learned a variety of actions and attitudes to help you avoid being a micromanager. At the same time, you learned several ideas for effective delegation.

18

How to Resolve Conflict

In this lesson you will learn several effective ways of resolving conflict, an activity that occupies approximately 20 percent of most leaders' time.

 Conflict A conflict is a situation in which two or more goals, values, or events are incompatible or mutually exclusive.

Confrontation and Problem Solving

The ideal approach to problem solving is to confront the real issue or underlying cause and then solve the problem. Confrontation means taking a problem-solving approach to differences and identifying facts, logic, or emotions that account for them. When you seek to resolve conflicts through confronting and understanding their causes, people feel responsible for the soundest solution. As a leader, you want long-lasting solutions to conflicts.

Confrontation can proceed gently, in a way that preserves a good working relationship. Suppose you are a department manager. Jaime, the manager of another department within your company, makes frequent attempts to recruit your most talented people. If you don't bring the problem to Jaime's attention, you fear Jaime will intensify his recruiting, thus depleting your department of talent. Yet you are hesitant to enter into an argument about an activity that the organization doesn't forbid.

A psychologically sound alternative is to use confrontation and problem solving. Here is an overview of the technique, followed by a step-by-step analysis. You approach Jaime directly in this manner:

> *You*: Jaime, there is something bothering me. I would like to discuss it with you.

> *Jaime*: Go ahead. I don't mind listening to other people's problems.

> *You*: My problem concerns something you are doing that makes it difficult for me to run my department smoothly. When you frequently attempt to entice my strongest team members to join your department, it disturbs me. Maybe I'm overly ethical, but I don't think what you are doing is just.

> *Jaime*: I never thought that offering people good job opportunities was unethical. But in the future, I will clear it with you first before talking to one of your team members about an opportunity in my department.

(Notice that you have probably enhanced your leadership stature with Jaime because of the productive way in which you approached the conflict.)

In more detail, confrontation and problem solving consist of six steps:

1. Awareness. Party A recognizes that a conflict exists between himself or herself and Party B.

2. The decision to confront the issue. Party A decides that the conflict is serious enough to justify a confrontation with Party B and that such a confrontation is preferable to avoiding the conflict.

3. The confrontation. Party A decides to handle the conflict in a problem-solving manner and confronts Party B. At this point, Party B may indicate a willingness to accept the confrontation or may decide to gloss over its seriousness. Often the conflict is resolved at this step, particularly if it is not serious and complicated.

4. Determining the cause of the conflict. The two parties discuss their respective opinions, attitudes, and feelings in regard to the conflict and attempt to identify the real issue. For example, the real cause of the issue between the two department managers was a difference of opinion about the ethics of internal recruiting methods.

5. Deciding on actions to reduce conflict. In this step the parties attempt to develop specific means of reducing or eliminating the cause of the conflict. If the cause can't be changed (such as a difference of opinion about the best way to do a particular task) the parties devise a way of working around the cause. If both parties agree on a solution, the confrontation has been successful.

6. Follow-up. After they implement the solution, both parties should check periodically to determine if the agreements they made have been kept. For example, if you have agreed that a person should complete a task as he or she sees fit, check in with one another to see if you are getting the results you both want. If not, work together to devise methods for improvement.

INVENT OPTIONS FOR MUTUAL GAIN

The most long-lasting solution to conflict is to develop alternative solutions that satisfy the interests of both parties. Options that result in gains for both sides are referred to as win-win solutions because both sides win something important. If the solution is too one-sided, the conflict will probably re-emerge. An effective leader is concerned about finding options for mutual gain because a major purpose of leadership is to unite people.

Here is an example of inventing an option for mutual gain: Workers in a small company wanted a three percent across-the-board salary increase. They believed their compensation was below that of workers in comparable companies. The president and company owner said she couldn't afford to increase salaries because the additional expense would virtually eliminate profits. The workers' representatives said that several of the best employees would quit if an across-the-board increase wasn't granted.

After mulling over the problem for a day, the president exercised leadership. She told the workers that they would be eligible for the three percent increase under one condition. They would have to find ways to cover the money for the compensation boost by increasing productivity and decreasing waste. The workers accepted the challenge and rose to the occasion. As a result, the workers received the additional pay and the company was able to stay profitable.

When attempting to invent options for mutual gain, consider the following suggestions:

- Keep reminding yourself and the other side that the outcome of conflict resolution isn't inevitably one position winning out over the other.

- Generate several workable options before entering the conflict-resolution session. The negotiation session could be so stressful that it will be difficult to think creatively.

- Ask the other party also to brainstorm possible solutions for mutual gain before the negotiation session.

- Shortly after the conflict-resolution session begins, make a statement to the effect, "I'm glad we're together working on this problem. I'm confident we'll find a way to protect both our interests."

- Don't be discouraged if an option for mutual gain doesn't come to mind immediately. Very few negotiators are quick to invent options for mutual gains.

HAVE BOTH SIDES EXCHANGE DEMANDS

Another constructive method of resolving conflict is for both sides to exchange demands. The sides could be two individuals, a representative from each side, or two groups attempting to resolve the conflict. Each side should develop a checklist or complete written description of what it wants the other side to do.

The lists are then exchanged and pondered carefully. As a result of studying the demands included on a list, useful compromises are often reached. Suppose a software company is in conflict with a computer manufacturer over a royalty agreement for using its operating system in the computer. Here are two examples of demands and possible compromises:

- "You say you need .75 percent royalty on the wholesale price of every computer we sell. Could you live with .50 percent for the first 50,000 units sold, and .75 percent on all those beyond that number?"

- "You say you want exclusive rights to the use of our operating software in your computers. We would be willing to grant exclusivity if you sell a minimum of 100,000 units the first year. If you don't reach that figure, we would then attempt to license our software to at least one other computer manufacturer."

Find Out What the Other Person Wants A quick way to resolve conflict with another individual is to ask, "What do you want me to do?" When asked this question many people will respond with a less extreme demand than their initial position.

USE COGNITIVE RESTRUCTURING

An indirect way of resolving conflict with others is to lessen the conflict-laden elements in a situation by viewing them more positively. Cognitive restructuring enables you to convert negative aspects into positive ones by looking for positive elements in a situation.

 Cognitive Restructuring   Cognitive restructuring is a method of mentally converting negative aspects into positive ones by looking for the positive elements in a situation.

How you frame or choose your thoughts can determine the outcome of a conflict. Your thoughts influence your actions. If you search for the beneficial aspects in the situation, there will be less area for dispute. Although this technique might sound like a mind game to you, it can work effectively.

Imagine that your boss, Kyle, has been asking you repeated questions about minute aspects of your operation. You are about ready to tell Kyle, "Can't you leave me alone? I don't like being micromanaged as if I'm a new trainee."

Instead, you look for the positive elements in the situation. You say to yourself, "Kyle has been asking me a lot of questions. This takes time, but answering these questions has merit. It keeps my boss informed and it makes me think through my work processes. An effective leader must meet the demands of all his or her constituents."

After having completed the cognitive restructuring, you can then deal with the conflict situation more positively. You might tell your boss, "I welcome the opportunity to review the details of my operation. Yet could we schedule these reviews at a time so they interfere less with the smooth functioning of my group?"

HANDLE CRITICISM CONSTRUCTIVELY

A substantial amount of conflict in the workplace arises from one person criticizing another. As a leader, you are or will be criticized frequently. Leaders who benefit from criticism are able to stand outside themselves while being criticized. It is as if they are watching the criticism from a distance and looking for its possible merits. Leaders who take criticism personally agonize when receiving negative feedback.

 Let the Other Side Simmer Down   In attempting to resolve conflict, you will occasionally encounter an individual who is so angry and irrational that working out a solution to the problem seems impossible. Let the person rant until he or she calms down, then attempt to solve the problem. Or come back the next day.

In this lesson you learned different strategies and tactics for resolving the conflict that a leader inevitably faces.

19

How to Help Others Think More Creatively

In this lesson you will learn how to encourage creative problem solving among group members. Encouraging creativity is important for leaders because they are supposed to bring about change and innovation.

 Creativity Creativity is the process of developing new ideas that can be put into action.

Establish Innovation Goals for the Team

The primary approach to enhancing creativity and innovation would be for you, as leader, to establish innovation goals for the team. In essence, you tell the team, "Our mandate is to be innovative" or "We must develop at least three dramatically improved work processes this year." Creativity and innovation are not synonyms. Some experts, however, regard creativity as imaginative thinking that leads to innovation or ideas that can be put to use.

Simply telling people to be innovative and establishing goals that require innovation is likely to foster at least some innovation. Yet this approach is really too mechanistic and too shallow to bring any dramatic results. Leaders who achieve genuine innovations engage in a variety of practices that stimulate creativity.

Not every leader who is successful at fostering innovation engages consistently in all of the activities reviewed here. Yet the more of these activities and attitudes you incorporate into your repertoire, the greater the chance that you will encourage innovation among your team members.

DEVELOP A PERMISSIVE ATMOSPHERE

The most influential step a manager can take to bring about creative problem solving is to develop a permissive atmosphere. A permissive atmosphere contributes to innovation because it encourages people to think freely and take intellectual risks. At the same time, group members must feel that they won't be penalized for making honest mistakes.

Microsoft Corporation is a stellar example of an organization in which leaders encourage workers at all levels to pursue their imagination. It was a relatively low-ranking member of the organization who dared tell top management that they were behind the times by not developing Internet-related products. The suggestion led to quick actions that have made Microsoft a dominant player in providing Internet services.

Here is a sampling of actions and techniques that contribute to a permissive, creativity-enhancing atmosphere:

- Consistently ask group members challenging questions such as "How would you solve this problem?" "What fresh ideas can you offer me?"

- Reinforce your quest for imaginative thinking with statements such as "Give me a few wild ideas on how to approach this problem. In this preliminary stage of our thinking, no idea is too off-the-wall." (A statement of this nature subtly communicates the point that you won't ridicule any idea. One reason many people don't make their potentially innovative ideas public is that they fear ridicule.)

- Let group members know when you have implemented a creative idea.

- Give recognition to good ideas by mentioning them in e-mail messages and during staff meetings.

- Minimize penalizing mistakes stemming from implementing imaginative alternative solutions to problems. Creativity is a numbers game in which the vast majority of ideas fail.

- Loosen up on financial controls. Financial controls contribute to organizational success.

ACCEPT PARTIALLY DEVELOPED IDEAS

Another creativity-encouraging tactic is for the leader to accept partially developed ideas. Managers of productive research laboratories listen to and support half-formed proposals and encourage team members to develop their ideas. Leaders in other disciplines should also avoid nipping innovation in the bud by discouraging the flow of ideas.

During a corporate downsizing, a staff member suggested that the company reduce costs by eliminating all customer-service centers in the field. Several of the other staff members laughed, but the president said, "You might be on to something. Why not play with your ideas further?"

Playing with the suggestion for closing customer-service centers eventually led to the closing of ten low-traffic centers. The company maintained a local telephone listing in the cities where the offices were closed. Local calls were automatically routed by telephone equipment to a central location. When problems couldn't be fixed over the phone, the company dispatched a customer-service technician within 72 hours to visit the customer's site.

GIVE FEEDBACK AND FINANCIAL REWARDS FOR SUCCESSFUL INNOVATIONS

A leader can also encourage innovation by giving positive feedback when an innovation succeeds. Innovation is its own reward to some extent. Nevertheless, creative problem solvers still enjoy knowing the specifics about how their idea made a contribution.

It's also a good idea to supplement verbal feedback about innovative suggestions with financial rewards. Innovators, like most workers, appreciate financial rewards. The financial reward tells the innovators in specific terms that you and the company value their contribution and are willing to pay for it. It also reflects recognition of outstanding performance. Various approaches to giving financial rewards for innovation include:

- Employee suggestion programs with financial payouts.
- Rewarding innovators with a small percentage of the profits stemming from their innovations.

- Including creative problem solving in performance reviews, thereby basing salary increases partially on innovation.

BE WILLING TO STRETCH ORGANIZATIONAL POLICY

A willingness to stretch organizational policy is another way to foster innovation. Managers must know when to stretch company policy to launch an idea. One example would be spending unused travel-budget money to help purchase equipment needed to develop a prototype for a new product. Another would be using travel money to purchase books, journals, and newsletters as sources of ideas.

BE WILLING TO MAKE QUICK DECISIONS

An ability and willingness to make quick decisions contributes to an atmosphere in which innovative activities can flourish. Leaders who foster creativity can spot a good idea and decide quickly whether to use organizational resources to develop it. The willingness to respond quickly to good ideas is important because creative people are eager to see their ideas translated into action.

BROADEN YOUR OUTLOOK AND THAT OF YOUR STAFF

If you are a leader who wants to encourage innovation, it's helpful to broaden your outlook and that of your staff, too.

Innovative thinking is often hampered because people are thinking only about the job at hand. Try these suggestions for broadening your outlook:

- Bring in outsiders to talk with you and your staff. The most important requirement is that the outsider be a person who can generate a fresh perspective. Many retired senior executives are eager to talk with a new generation of employees. Drawing on their past successes, they can sometimes inspire employees to think in fresh ways.

- Bring in someone who is an expert on a topic of interest to your staff. This might or might not be directly job related. An expert in storytelling might stimulate your group to think imaginatively, for example.

- Devote a portion of an occasional staff meeting to what could be termed "Sparkling Ideas from the Outside World." Group members can bring in ideas found by reading books and magazines or by talking with other people. The goal should be to import any idea that reflects imaginative thinking.

A broadened or fresh perspective is important for another reason. Lack of innovation stems from a narrow outlook, such as thinking that prompt delivery is important to all customers. (Some standards may be generally true, but to think that any practice is *always* the most appropriate is a narrow outlook.)

ENCOURAGE A HUNGER FOR IDEAS

A robust method of creating an innovation-friendly environment is for the leader to encourage a hunger for ideas. Creative people characteristically seek out new ideas constantly, both on and off the job. They scan large amounts of printed and electronic information to come away with a few nuggets that might lead to the commercialization of an idea. The manager can contribute to the development of an idea-hungry group by such steps as:

- Asking periodically, "What idea have you read, seen, or heard lately than can help us?"

- Bringing in useful ideas himself or herself from time to time to serve as an example of idea hunting.

- Periodically committing an entire staff meeting to sharing new and potentially useful ideas.

- Conducting a best-idea-of-the-quarter contest by asking the group to rate on a 1-to-10 scale about a dozen of what you consider to be the most useful ideas submitted during the quarter. The winning idea would be the one that receives the highest average rating from the group.

Make Regular Use of Brainstorming

Brainstorming is a well-known technique for shaking loose alternative solutions to a problem. Quite often the ideas emerging from the brainstorming session have to be refined later. Brainstorming is typically conducted in groups, but the results may be just as good when individuals brainstorm by themselves.

Brainstorming Brainstorming is a technique for quickly generating several ideas, no matter how unusual or unworkable initially, to address a problem or look for new opportunities.

Another brainstorming option is the electronic variety in which group members enter their ideas into a computer. Ideas submitted by each group member are instantly flashed on the screen of the other group members.

It's important for the leader to emphasize brainstorming for two reasons: Brainstorming helps find creative solutions to problems, while at the same time enhancing the creative problem-solving skills of participants.

Press for More Alternative Solutions The essence of creative thinking is to find multiple potential solutions to a problem. When a group member brings you one solution to a problem,and you don't regard it as outstanding, say to him or her, "OK, what other suggestions can you offer?"

IMPLEMENT OTHER CREATIVE PROBLEM-SOLVING TECHNIQUES

Brainstorming is wellknown, yet other techniques derived from brainstorming do an equally good job of solving problems and encouraging creativity. One of the most effective, and enjoyable, is the pet-peeve technique. The purpose of this technique is to challenge the status quo and critically examine what features of your operation your internal and external customers might not like. The following activities are involved in the pet-peeve technique:

- Through group discussion, team members develop a list of complaints others might have of your group. Sources of complaints include inside customers, outside customers, competitors, and suppliers.

- During group discussion (or brainstorming), the group throws in some imaginary and some humorous complaints. No holds are barred.

- Group members are allowed to prepare for the meeting by soliciting feedback from the various target groups. The feedback should be conducted informally, in keeping with the informal, breezy style of the pet-peeve group.

- The humorous complaints are especially important because humor releases creativity. (An underwriting group in an insurance company listed this pet peeve: "We're known as the policy prevention group because we turn down all the wonderful potential customers the sales reps bring to us.")

- After all the complaints have been aired, plans are drawn to remedy the most serious problems.

In this lesson you learned some leadership actions that will foster the right atmosphere for creative thinking. You also learned several specific techniques to enhance creative problem solving.

How to Lead Group Members Toward Exceptional Quality

In this lesson you will learn principles and techniques to help you to lead group members toward attaining high-quality goods and services.

Contribute to a Corporate Culture of Quality

Top-level executives have the primary responsibility for creating a corporate culture that fosters high-quality work throughout the organization. If the corporate culture doesn't embody quality, any quality improvement efforts will probably be shallow and short lived. World-class quality companies such as Motorola and Waterman (writing instruments) operate in a culture of quality.

Leaders below the level of top management are responsible for sustaining the culture of quality developed at the top. One of the dominant values of a culture of quality is continuous improvement. Leaders who are close to the operations of an organization are in the best position to foster continuous improvement, or *kaizen*. A leader can encourage continuous improvements by such means as:

- Encouraging workers to stay alert for possible small improvements.

- Asking workers to look for situations that aren't quite right, but are not yet full-blown problems.

- Telling group members frequently that "tweaking" of techniques and work processes is valuable.

- Explaining to group members that hitting a home run is laudable, but just getting a base hit is also valuable to the organization.

- Commenting positively about minor improvements spearheaded by group members.

Kaizen Kaizen is a Japanese word meaning gradual and continuous improvement in personal and work life as well as in the quality of products and services. Over time, the compounded results of this effort result in dramatic improvements for everyone.

Following the other eight principles and techniques explained in this lesson also contributes directly or indirectly to a culture of quality.

BUILD QUALITY INTO THE TEAM MISSION STATEMENT

When you incorporate quality into the team mission statement, workers have another strong reminder of the importance of quality. The mission statement should make reference to quality. Two examples of team mission statements that include quality are as follows:

- To provide such a high-quality level of customer service that our customers will hold us in high regard, and that we will develop an excellent reputation in our industry.

- To provide such high-quality printing and reproduction services to the rest of the organization that outside vendors for these services won't be needed.

INVOLVE AND EMPOWER EMPLOYEES

To achieve quality management, leaders must empower employees to fix and prevent problems. Equally important, group members have to accept the authority and become involved in the improvement process. Involvement and empowerment include actions such as:

- Clustering employees into quality-improvement teams to search for ways to improve product, services, and the processes by which work gets accomplished.

- Asking employees regularly how the organizational unit can function even better.

- Granting customer-service workers more latitude than they had previously to resolve customer problems.

- Encouraging employees to be the judge of their own quality rather than relying on another organizational unit to check their quality.

Listen to Employees

A successful quality-improvement effort creates an atmosphere in which the manager listens to employees. Management by walking around is therefore standard practice in a high-quality organization. Managers should listen for suggestions about even minor aspects of quality.

Weyerhauser Mortgage of Woodland Hills, California, was experiencing delays in receiving reimbursement checks from FHA-insured home loans. Team members contended that company mistakes in completing forms were the culprit—not the government. The company listened and eliminated the mistakes. The checks began arriving in one-sixth the time, resulting in substantial savings.

Immerse Group Members in Quality

A leader can spearhead quality within the work unit following a method often used to learn a second language—the immersion technique. The idea is to get group members studying quality and talking about it frequently. People in your sphere of influence should be asked to read informative books and articles about quality, watch videos on the topic, and access information about quality online. Reading and study should be followed up with small-group discussion, with such questions as the following:

- How do we as a firm (or organizational unit) stack up against the companies we just read about?

- After reading the article or book, what are our strengths, weaknesses, and opportunities?

- Where do we need to go? What are our plans for getting there?

CLOSE THE QUALITY CREDIBILITY GAP

Many firms talk about quality but few follow through with rigorously enforced plans to achieve it. An important leadership technique is to close the credibility gap—the difference between the message employees hear and the actual follow-through. A survey conducted by the American Society for Quality Control revealed an average credibility gap of almost 20 percent. To close the credibility gap, leaders can take such actions as:

- Accepting a late penalty rather than shipping a defective product.

- Including high-quality results as a factor in promotion.

- Demoting a high-level manager whose unit achieves consistently poor quality.

- Getting in touch with customers who make extremely negative complaints on customer satisfaction surveys.

INSIST THAT GROUP MEMBERS FIGURE OUT HOW TO ACHIEVE EXTRAORDINARY QUALITY GOALS

A bold quality-enhancing leadership practice is to establish extraordinarily difficult quality targets for group members. You then insist that they figure out a way to attain them. Without revamping the current work process, pursuing an extraordinarily difficult goal might simply lead to frustration.

The manager of commercial mortgages at a bank might tell the group that mortgage applications must now be completed in four working days. At present the process might take an average of 22 working days. A group member will inevitably say, "It can't be done." The leader might reply, "You are right. It can't be done *if you process mortgages the way our bank always has*."

As the leader, you further inspire the group by telling them they are free to challenge any company rule or procedure that blocks the achievement of the extraordinary goal. You might even discover that getting approvals from you along the way is one of the impediments to quick accomplishment.

EMPHASIZE THE HUMAN SIDE OF QUALITY

Statistical and problem-solving techniques contribute heavily to quality improvement. Yet the real thrust of quality management is for all employees to have positive attitudes toward quality. They must pay attention to detail, take pride in their work, and believe that high quality improves profits. To emphasize the human side of quality, attempt to influence group members with reminders such as:

- Every product, service, or process you work on is a partial self-portrait. It tells the person who uses your output something important about your character.

- You can't achieve high quality without being highly conscientious.

- Imagine you are a passenger on a commercial airliner or that a loved one is having brain surgery. How much attention to detail would be appropriate for that pilot or surgeon?

- Attempt to achieve that same amount of attention to detail when you perform work for other company employees or customers.

REWARD HIGH-QUALITY PERFORMANCE

The best quality results are likely to be achieved when employees receive internal as well as external rewards for achieving quality. Internal rewards include such factors as

- The joy of doing quality work.

- Pride in accomplishment.

- The inner satisfaction of doing things right the first time.

- The avoidance of the frustration associated with rework.

The external rewards for quality include such factors as salary increases, cash bonuses, recognition plaques, banquets, and certificates for quality achievement. And don't forget that positive feedback, including a warm smile and approval, remains one of the most powerful external rewards at a leader's disposal.

Hold Frequent Quality Reviews   A quick and direct way to improve and sustain quality is to have periodic reviews of what your unit did right and wrong from a quality standpoint. When discussing what went wrong, avoid finger pointing— just get the group focused on the problem's cause and take action that will prevent it from happening in the future.

INDEX